The Trouble with Buddhism

How the Buddhist tradition has betrayed its own insights

Robert M. Ellis

Published in the UK by Robert M. Ellis,
copyright 2011
Printed and distributed by Lulu.com
ISBN 978-1-4475-1678-1

By the same author:

A Theory of Moral Objectivity
A New Buddhist Ethics
Truth on the Edge

Up to date information on publications, supporting material, and a discussion forum are available on the website
http://www.moralobjectivity.net

The author can be emailed on
re@moralobjectivity.net

The Trouble with Buddhism

How the Buddhist tradition has betrayed its own insights

By Robert M. Ellis

I bid you remain true to earth, my brethren, with the power of your virtue! Let your giving love and your knowledge serve the meaning of earth! Thus I beg and conjure you.
Let it not flee from what is earthly and beat with its wings against eternal walls! Alas, how much virtue hath ever so flown and gone astray!
         Nietzsche *Thus Spake Zarathustra*

If you meet the Buddha on the road, kill him.
         Zen proverb

Contents

INTRODUCTION 7
    A NOTE ON "BUDDHISM" 12

CHAPTER 1: THE FOUR NOBLE PRINCIPLES 17
    THE MIDDLE WAY 17
    THE THREE MARKS OF CONDITIONED EXISTENCE 25
    GREED AND HATRED 39
    THE POSSIBILITY OF PROGRESS 48
    THE FOUR NOBLE PRINCIPLES 54

CHAPTER 2: THE SOURCES OF JUSTIFIED BELIEF IN BUDDHISM 55
    THE CONFUSING OF SOURCES OF KNOWLEDGE IN BUDDHISM 55
    JUSTIFIED BELIEFS FROM THE MIDDLE WAY 63
    THE TROUBLE WITH BUDDHIST METAPHYSICS 70
    THE TROUBLE WITH GURUS 80
    THE TROUBLE WITH SCRIPTURES 85

CHAPTER 3: THE CONSTRAINT OF COMPASSION 96
    THE CULTIVATION OF LOVE 96
    THE CONSTRAINT OF THE IDEAL 100
    THE DIVISION OF LOVE 105
    SELF AND EGO 111

CHAPTER 4: THE TROUBLE WITH KARMA 120
    COSMIC HOUSE POINTS 120
    KARMA VS NIRVANA 132
    RIDICULOUS REBIRTH 137
    BUDDHISM WITHOUT KARMA 146

CHAPTER 5: THE TROUBLE WITH CONDITIONALITY 149
    THE TWELVE LINKS 149

THE GENERAL PRINCIPLE OF DEPENDENT ORIGINATION 156
MUTUAL CAUSALITY AND INTERDEPENDENCY 160

CHAPTER 6: THE TROUBLE WITH REALITY ... 166

IT'S ALL IN THE MIND 167
THE EMPTINESS OF THE EMPTINESS OF EMPTINESS 173
REALITY IS HERE AND NOW 177
QUANTUM IRRELEVANCIES 180
NUGATORY NATURE 184

CHAPTER 7: BUDDHA TROUBLE 188

SYMBOL AND RITUAL 188
WARTS AND TOPKNOTS 194
BUDDHA GONE BAROQUE 198
MANDALAS AND LOTUSES 205

CHAPTER 8: DHARMA TROUBLE 213

WASN'T IT TRUE ALL THE TIME? 214
PUTTING IT IN CONTEXT 218
RIGHTEOUS CHRISTIANS AND HOLY HINDUS 223
OVERSOLD TOLERANCE 227

CHAPTER 9: SANGHA TROUBLE 234

THE TROUBLE WITH MONASTICISM 234
THE TROUBLE WITH ORDERS 241
THE BUDDHIST SOCIETY OF FRIENDS 245

CHAPTER 10: THE ETHICS INDUSTRY 250

PURGE AND PURIFY 250
MEMORISE THE REGULATIONS 253
FOLLOW THE PRECEPTS 258
SKILFUL MEANS 263
THE ACADEMICS MOVE IN 267

CHAPTER 11: THE MEDITATION BAZAAR 270

MEDITATION AS AN END IN ITSELF 270
INSTANT ENLIGHTENMENT 275

SECRET SADHANAS 277
MANTRIC MUMBO-JUMBO 281

CHAPTER 12: THE DOOR OF WISDOM IS LOCKED 284

I HAVEN'T UNPACKED YET 286
I KEEP REPEATING MYSELF 291
I NEED AN UPDATE 294
I'VE GOT CULTURE-SHOCK 295
I'M QUITE FAMILIAR REALLY 298

CONCLUSION 302

Introduction

The title of this book might suggest a rant by a disillusioned ex-Buddhist: but this is not the intention. Although I am no longer personally committed to the Buddhist tradition, I am still committed to practising its central insights. I want to use those insights to try to separate the wheat from the chaff in traditional Buddhism. This is a critical book about Buddhism from a perspective which is still sympathetic to some of its central teachings.

After around twenty years of engagement in Buddhism, I have reached the conclusion that Buddhism has largely betrayed its own insights. On the other hand, those insights are still there, and there is much that is valuable to be learned from Buddhism. Personally, I am no longer sure whether I should describe myself as a "Buddhist" or not, because it all depends whether this is taken to mean that I am committed to the core insights of the Middle Way (which I am) or to Buddhism as a tradition (which I am not).

I am writing this book not just to try to get Buddhists to look more radically at the defects in their own religion, but also to help both Buddhists and non-Buddhists to differentiate those defects from what is valuable. We should celebrate Buddhism's insights, whilst decrying their betrayal. My main emphasis is a critical one, because I want to get people to think again about things they have taken for granted in Buddhism, but that doesn't mean the intention is negative.

There are many Westerners approaching Buddhism today and finding much that is positive there. On first encountering Buddhism myself, one of the first things that I found impressive was the people. Sometimes years of practice can give Buddhist leaders an integrity, straightforwardness and trustworthiness that are certainly far beyond anything I have met elsewhere. Another impressive feature is the thinking. Buddhism in the West is a young religion, and there is still lots of real thinking and experimentation going on. Far from settling into a niche and just defending their position, as religionists often do, Western Buddhists are often still debating what they should believe and how they should live. For me this gives the Buddhist community a sense of openness and vitality that is valuable.

Buddhism focuses on practice, on changing the individual for the better; unlike too many other religions which either focus solely on belief, or on performing rituals that help to give a community its identity but have little further value. Many of its meditation practices are accessible to all, whether or not they think themselves "Buddhist", and many people in the West are benefiting from them.

However, these positive features are unfortunately accompanied by others that often stop newcomers in their tracks, or confront them with quite reasonable doubts after only a little while. Despite its emphasis on practicality, Buddhism is still tied to an Eastern tradition that interferes with that practical value. The openness and practicality is obstructed by piles of dogma shipped in from Asian cultures. Many Buddhist teachings that at first appear plausible, when examined more closely, turn out to be contradictory. These contradictions are often mistaken for mystical insights when they are nothing of the kind.

Buddhists sometimes criticise Christianity for its reliance on belief in God and the revelations of the Bible. Yet Buddhist belief in the revelations of the Buddha from his enlightened state is often comparable in ways that many Buddhists seem unwilling to recognise. The strong tradition of faith in the guru also raises similar worries. Many schools of Buddhism maintain a tradition of monasticism that separates Buddhists into first and second-class categories, whilst even those Buddhists who have given up monasticism often maintain a sentimental attachment to the idea of it. Similarly, with karma and rebirth, even those Buddhists with apparently new interpretations of these traditional doctrines often turn out to have a strong sentimental attachment to them. Above all, much Buddhism turns out to be obsessed with an ideal of nirvana that is celebrated for its own sake, at the expense of the spiritual progression within ordinary experience that most commonly attracts people to Buddhist practice.

None of these kinds of worries would matter so much if Buddhists did not go so much out of their way to appear reasonable on the surface, thus creating a deceptive impression. In fact, their most vital, important, and insightful teachings often serve to lure people into Buddhism so that they then feel subsequently driven to swallow the dogmatic, traditional and unreasonable bits of Buddhism for fear of losing the good bits. Some teachings, like that of the ultimate emptiness of all phenomena in Mahayana Buddhism, seem to serve primarily to reassure the critical parts of Buddhist brains and make them feel their doubts have been addressed, when they have not at all. A general reassurance that everything is empty, endlessly repeated in scripture and ritual, does not get us anywhere in coming to terms with this fact and actually seeing its implications.

In becoming an ordained Buddhist, a member of the Western Buddhist Order, my experience was that I was obliged to either take Buddhism or leave it. Either one accepted the unhelpful bits of Buddhism with the helpful, or one did not get the benefit of the helpful. I did not want to lose the beneficial aspects of Buddhism, so I took ordination. Three years later, I realised that this had been a mistake: I had compromised my intellectual integrity by committing myself to Buddhist tradition, in a way that was in fact undermining my relationship to truth, and thus in the long run even undermining my ability to engage with the helpful practices of Buddhism. So I resigned from the Western Buddhist Order.

It should not be necessary for people like me in the West to face this dilemma. All that Buddhism needs to do is to reform itself in accordance with its core insights, and be ready to discard much of the other stuff that has been deposited on those insights to obscure them over the centuries. For Western Buddhists this would be relatively easy to do, for the tradition in the West has scarcely put down roots yet and could easily be shaped anew. It does not need to completely abandon doctrine, symbol and ritual, but it does need to give them a much more thorough overhaul than has yet been undertaken, even by apparently radical reformers such as Sangharakshita or Chögyam Trungpa. If this could be achieved then Buddhism could become much more clearly a force for good.

So what follows is an attempt to sort out what is useful in Buddhism from what is not useful, as the basis of a plea for reform much more radical than anything that has yet been attempted.

A note on "Buddhism"

Throughout this book one of the central issues is likely to be the nature of what I am criticising: what is Buddhism? Buddhists have become Buddhists for all kinds of different personal motives, and many have arrived at their own interpretations of what "Buddhism" means. The concept, is, of course, contested.

For most academics writing about Buddhism, statements about Buddhism need to be backed up by copious reference to scriptures, anthropological observations of Buddhist practice, or both. This approach, however, in no way leaves the idea of "Buddhism" any less contested; moreover the scriptures appealed to are often open to multiple interpretations, and are interpreted in line with the preconceptions that have gained currency in the small world of academic Buddhist studies. Appeals to scripture tend to lead one in the direction of complex and often fruitless arguments that are largely about the history and culture in which the scriptures were written, or the conditions of their production, not about universal human concerns. I will say more about this issue in the last section of chapter 2.

My approach to "Buddhism", to cut through this type of fruitless argument, will be simply to make statements about it based on my own experience, and examine their consistency. This method is philosophical, and in philosophy one makes progress, not by referring to sources of authority, but by investigating the grounds, consistency and implications of beliefs.

The experience that is my starting point consists in about twenty years of involvement with the Friends of the Western Buddhist Order (FWBO – recently renamed the Triratna Buddhist Community) plus some wider academic study of Buddhism. I will try to give due recognition to the diversity of opinion as I understand it, and not merely represent Buddhism in its "straw man" form of the most conservative versions. If anything, my impression is that I have been involved in one of the more radical sections of the Buddhist world, and will probably go further in accommodating some of the alternative approaches that are to be found in the FWBO than other more traditional Buddhists may find necessary.

There will be some limited discussion of scriptures where these are of particular importance, but I do not see any need or use in the academic practice of referencing all factual statements about Buddhism to a scripture. Rather this practice often distracts attention from the kinds of underlying problems I will be trying to address in this book, and for many gives a misleading sense of reassurance of the grounds of belief.

Obviously, the kind of Buddhism I will be addressing is a representative, broadly recognised one. In the vast majority of cases, I expect that this will largely fit with the experience of (Western or Westernised) readers with any experience of Buddhism. If you have so far customised Buddhism that my picture it does not fit with your understanding of Buddhism, then I congratulate you on having already done a lot of the kind of independent thinking I seek to stimulate in this book. For many years, I have myself worked with such a "customised" Buddhism, but also found distinct drawbacks in attempting to maintain a version of "Buddhism" which had little to do with what most other people thought it was. There comes a point where the strain of trying to hold such a position becomes too great, and perhaps one has to let go of the long-nurtured label "Buddhist".

In my experience, Buddhists often deny that criticisms of Buddhism are relevant to the Buddhism they follow, because of their belief that the true Dharma is wordless, beyond mere descriptions, and certainly not to be encompassed by the crudities of any description of "Buddhism". The purpose of this book is not to try to criticise any such true Dharma, if it exists. Instead, however, I would like Buddhists to start taking responsibility for the ways in which Buddhism is actually commonly explained and described, before they take refuge in idealisations.

Chapter 1: The four noble principles

The Middle Way

Expositions of Buddhism often start with the Four Noble Truths as the most basic teaching of Buddhism. That is one reason why I feel a need to address them from the beginning. Yet I cannot take the Four Noble Truths as they are normally presented and build on those, for even here, at the very starting point of Buddhism, there are confusions to clear up. These confusions suggest to me that the Buddhist betrayal of its own insights is no recent phenomenon, but started very early on in its history or was perhaps even there in confusions from the beginning. My main purpose, however, is not to try to trace the history of this betrayal, but simply to ask whether core Buddhist teachings are coherent and consistent, whether they make sense, and whether they are helpful in assisting people in the modern world to improve their lives.

Before examining the Four Noble Truths, I will need to establish an approach with which to examine them. The standard of judgement I will be applying is one which Buddhists often appeal to but which they apply incompletely: that of practical spiritual usefulness, of making people's lives better. This does not mean any attempt to reduce Buddhism to science, utilitarianism, postmodernism or any other modern Western doctrine, but to take the account of usefulness pointed to by central Buddhist teachings themselves.

The Buddhist teaching which is centrally concerned with usefulness is the Middle Way. We can assert this primarily through its role in the story of the life of the Buddha[1], a story that is of great symbolic value. It matters little how far it is historically true, much more how well it represents a core Buddhist insight.

Traditionally, the Buddha is said to have been a prince with an over-protective father, who sheltered him in the isolation of a palace from any kind of suffering and tried to distract him from any religious goal by surrounding him with pleasures. He was roused from the obsession with pleasure that

---

[1] There are many sources for the details of the Buddha's biography in the Buddhist tradition. In the Pali Canon, the *Ariyapariyesana Sutta* (Sutta 26, The Middle Length Discourses of the Buddha, trans. Ñanamoli and Bodhi, Wisdom 1995) gives important early elements of the story. It is more fully elaborated in the *Buddhacarita* of Ashvaghosha (ed. And trans. E.H.Johnston, Motilal Banarsidass 1972)

this sequestered existence symbolises through encounters with an old man, a sick man, a corpse, and a religious mendicant. Perhaps a modern equivalent to this might be a modern adolescent, lost in a highly protected technological world of instant gratification, suddenly finding himself in a developing country and confronted for the first time with the pains of common human experience as it has existed down the ages. As a result the purpose of his life changes.

The Buddha-to-be then dramatically renounces his protected and hedonistic lifestyle for the highly risky alternative of religious beggary. He leaves the palace and goes forth into the forest to seek enlightenment. At first he does this under the instruction of two different spiritual teachers, and then in company with a group of companions often known as the Five Ascetics. The Five Ascetics are trying to gain enlightenment through imposing pain and hardship upon themselves, in the belief that this can earn merit which they can subsequently cash out as enlightenment. The Buddha-to-be eventually realises, however, that this ascetic approach, too, is not conducive to enlightenment, but merely weakens his body. He abandons it, to the disgust of his companions.

The story so far has a symmetry. The Buddha-to-be has tried a life of pleasure and a life of pain, but neither approach has led to the enlightenment he sought. So he tries what subsequently became known as the Middle Way, and by this method, according to the traditional story, achieved enlightenment. The question of enlightenment is something we will unavoidably have to return to later in this book, but for me the story starts to become much less interesting at this point. What the Buddha finally achieved is of much less interest than the method he used to make progress towards it, because the method he used can be applied by anyone, anywhere, at any time, whereas there is nobody around who is verifiably enlightened. The story so far simply symbolises that method in a compelling narrative, but after this it starts making claims about the Buddha and about a state of nirvana which is both remote to us and in conception very much conditioned by Indian culture.

In my experience, Buddhists often go little further than saying that the Buddha followed the Middle Way between asceticism and self-indulgence. They might also discuss the Middle Way of beliefs which accompanies this: the Middle Way between eternalism (often defined as belief in an eternal self) and nihilism or annihilationism (often defined as the belief that the soul is cut off at death), which is extensively discussed in the Pali canon. They identify eternalism with asceticism and self-indulgence with nihilism, and point to Buddhist teaching as lying between these extremes. But they rarely go on to explain much more than this about the Middle Way, an incredibly rich teaching scandalously neglected by the religion that gave birth to it.

Yet the Middle Way, uniquely among central Buddhist teachings, is about how to generally go about judging the right way forward, rather than about some claimed state of affairs or about a more specific prescription for action. It is thus the only central Buddhist teaching which is completely universal, and which can be passed without reservation directly from the Buddha's ancient Indian context to a modern Western context. We do not have to worry about whether it is true and relevant today, because what it offers us is a general approach for working out what beliefs we should accept and what actions we should take *in any context*. We simply have to try it out in our own context, in a similar experimental fashion to the way in which the Buddha was said to have tried it out. In itself, it does not tell us to believe or to do anything, but if we make use of it, it will quite shortly make clear what we should believe and do in our context.

It does this basically by addressing conditions, not in a scientific way by creating positive theories about what will happen, but the other way round, by pointing out what approaches to conditions are likely to be mistaken and unhelpful. In a world that is constantly changing and always more complex than we take it to be or can readily grasp, it is overall certainties about the world or about how to act in it that are likely to be mistaken.

If we consider the religious, moral, and scientific certainties of the past – for example that sacrifices to the gods kept the world in order, that slavery is acceptable because master and slave classes are part of the world's design, or that the earth is at the centre of the universe – it seems clear that what may seem obvious at one time or place is not at another, and the less closely these theories could be checked through specific experiences, the more vulnerable they were to eventually being superseded. Let's take the idea that sacrifices to the gods maintained order. We can now see that this is mistaken because we can now see other, more concrete, ways, that we can experience more closely, which explain how the order of society can be maintained: for example, education, democracy, international institutions, and the police. Similarly, slavery is no longer acceptable because we can see that those who used to be slaves are in fact human beings with the same kinds of capabilities as those who used to be their masters, so that the justifications for giving them inferior status were mistaken. Both sacrifices and slavery were justified by *metaphysical* beliefs, i.e. beliefs that cannot even potentially be checked through experience of any kind.

It is dogmatic metaphysical claims of this kind that are unhelpful, because they lead us to make claims which stop us looking more carefully at people and events and becoming more closely aware of what they are actually like. In finding the Middle Way, the Buddha navigated between two types of metaphysical claim that were dominant in his time. One was the idea that there was an order in the universe that would ensure that every pain inflicted would be compensated in the future by pleasure hereafter, which we would continue to experience in an eternal existence (eternalism). The other was that we do not know of, or at least can safely ignore, any such order, and will cease to exist after death anyway, so we should just fall in with the values of those around us and get pleasure where we can (nihilism). It is by navigating between these extremes that he managed to engage with the conditions in his own life that were holding back his spiritual progression. The Middle Way helped him engage with the conditions created by the craving, hatred and ignorance of his own mind, which he could only address by combining disciplined strength of resolve with care for himself.

It was through following this Middle Way in his context that the Buddha managed to not only get closer to discovering the truth about himself and the world, but also find the values that would subsequently motivate him. To make this procedure universal, one should navigate between the metaphysical dogmas *of one's own time and place*, and thus attempt to engage with one's own conditions more closely, rather than assuming that one's navigation will be in any other respects similar to the Buddha's.

Before saying much more about this, however, we will first need to backtrack to say more about what are more generally considered to be the basic principles of Buddhism. I shall consider these in the light of the Middle Way as the most universal method, and try to assess whether these principles are indeed consistent with the Middle Way or not.

The three marks of conditioned existence

Many accounts of Buddhism start with the three *lakshanas*, or three marks (or characteristics) of conditioned existence: dukkha (unsatisfactoriness), anicca (impermanence) and anatta (insubstantiality). These are said to give a basic Buddhist analysis of the nature of phenomenal existence, and together form the First Noble Truth, at the root of Buddhist teaching[2]. They are also a good place to start in distinguishing the core principles of Buddhism.

Dukkha

The first mark of conditioned existence is *dukkha*. This has long been mistranslated as "suffering", even by Buddhists themselves, but it refers not just to the experience of pain or suffering as such, but also to the experience of loss or mortification when we do not experience an expected pleasure,

---

[2] For example, see Walpola Rahula, What the Buddha Taught (Wisdom 1990), or Sangharakshita A Guide to the Buddhist Path (Windhorse 1990) p.177

and to a more general sense of meaninglessness (*sankhara-dukkha*). What these doctrines have in common is the idea of *unsatisfactoriness*, i.e. the idea that our experience does not give us ultimate satisfaction, however promising it may appear.

Dukkha is a feature of *conditioned existence* or samsara, which means that what is being claimed is not that the universe itself is dukkha, just that the phenomenal universe (the universe we experience) is dukkha. But does this claim ring true? The whole of what I experience will only be unsatisfactory if I compare it to a standard of satisfaction that it fails to live up to, and clearly sometimes this happens. For example, I want this book to be accepted by a publisher, and I shall be disappointed and feel it to be unsatisfactory or frustrating if every publisher rejects it; but the reason for this is because I have a desire for the book to be published, a model in my mind of what will happen which may be disappointed. If I lacked this desire, however, I would feel no frustration, and would not experience the world as frustrating.

In order to maintain the belief that all phenomenal existence is *dukkha*, Buddhists must insist that I can never experience anything without this anticipation of satisfaction that is then not satisfied; or that if I do have such experiences of being free from dukkha, then I must be enlightened. But how do they know this? How do they know that everyone's experience is *always* unsatisfactory? How do they even know that their *own* experience is always unsatisfactory?

To test any claim we need to look at possible counter-examples. In this case, I try to imagine the most satisfying experience of my life to see whether I can make sense of the belief that it is ultimately unsatisfactory. What springs to mind are, for example, meditational experiences, experiences of achievement on completing a project, or experiences of sexual or sensual satisfaction. When I experienced all of these, was I somehow comparing them to a divine template, in comparison with which these "satisfying" experiences were unsatisfactory? I think not.

To insist that all these "satisfying" experiences must have been ultimately "unsatisfactory" not only requires skating over the experience itself and imposing a dogmatic framework on it, but it also means assuming that we will never have a fully satisfying experience in the future, short of enlightenment. As soon as we cease to trust

27

our own experience of satisfaction at the point we have that experience, dogma rears its head, because no matter what our experience might be, it will make no difference to the belief that it is unsatisfactory. We will then have no other standard by which to judge than the wholesale acceptance of the dogma that all experience is unsatisfactory. The doctrine of dukkha requires that everyone always has a perfect measure in mind beside which the world seems imperfect. Buddhists have no way of knowing that this is the case, and thus must dogmatically assert it. But they do not need to do so.

The useful insight to be found in the doctrine of dukkha has nothing to do with a claim about the phenomenal universe, let alone the actual universe. It is simply a claim that *if* we hold up a standard of perfect satisfaction as a basis of judging our experience (as we often, in fact, seem to do), we find that experience wanting. This means that if we want to stop experiencing dukkha, we should stop using this perfect measure. The principle is one about how we *should* see things, not how things are.

This point may be seen more clearly if we tried turning around the doctrine of dukkha and made it into a doctrine of *sukha*, or happiness. Supposing we claimed that everything in the phenomenal universe, all our experiences, was in fact happy. They might seem unhappy sometimes, but this is just because we are not using the right measure to judge what we experience. If we used the correct standard of imperfection, indeed of general grottiness in the universe, we would see that what we actually experience is always better than this. Since this is the true standard to judge by, it might be claimed, in fact the universe is much better than our expectations.

This doctrine of *sukha* is neither more nor less implausible than the doctrine of *dukkha*, Like dukkha, it says that *if* we apply a certain type of standard to our experience, that experience will be found wanting. What it doesn't do is show that we in fact always apply that standard, or even that we ought to. In practice, because our cravings often lead us to get attached to an idealisation of how things are going to be, dukkha is probably much more common than sukha, and that is why the doctrine of dukkha offers a useful insight for many people: but it does not give a universal law any more than *sukha* does.

Superficial critics of Buddhism often take the doctrine of dukkha to indicate pessimism, and Buddhists hasten to defend themselves against this charge by explaining that *dukkha* has a positive purpose. It does indeed have a positive purpose. If you don't identify a problem and acknowledge its existence, you cannot fix it, and dukkha provides a foundation for the positive progress offered in the other Noble Truths. However, this positive purpose is not furthered by taking dukkha to be a truth about the phenomenal universe. It would be better served by giving dukkha as a practical principle about how we should respond to the suffering we experience, pointing out the drawbacks of allowing craving to determine our way of seeing it.

So the first element of the "First Noble Truth" is not a *truth* at all. It does point to a useful insight, but one that has been misleadingly presented through the ages. Newcomers to Buddhism have to struggle to beat their way through the obfuscation of its traditional presentation in order to get to the useful teaching, and things are made unnecessarily difficult for them from the very beginning. It appears that Buddhism wants to deny, or at least underemphasise, the degree of positive fulfilment we do actually get from our imperfect existence, but it does not need to do this to make the underlying point. How many newcomers have been needlessly put off by this presentation of the "truth" at the beginning? Why does Buddhism continue to present itself in this misleading way? This is a question I will have many occasions to repeat in this book.

Anicca

Let us now look, a little more briefly, at the other two marks of conditioned existence. *Anicca*, the doctrine of impermanence, is again often expressed in the form that all conditioned things are impermanent. We suffer, in part, because we take what is actually impermanent to be permanent, not recognising its true nature.

Once again, though, when this is offered as a truth about conditioned existence we find that whether it is true depends on your standpoint. When we stand looking at a river, are we seeing continual change because the waters flow by, or an absence of change because the river is still there? Any experience over a given period of time will reveal some features that appear to change during that time and others which remain the same. Why should we focus on one of these features and not the other? To say that we should focus on change, not permanence, because the world is *really* changing rather than really permanent, is just dogmatic. My experience itself is not necessarily one of impermanence unless I judge it lacking by the measure of an absolute permanence, but there is no way of proving that this is always the measure I *really* apply, or really ought to apply, when there are other possible ways of seeing it.

For example, let's take the case of bereavement. This is the classic case of impermanence often mentioned by Buddhists. It is claimed that we assume people to be permanent: then, when they are taken away from us by death, we suffer because we are not adapted to the impermanence of the universe. No doubt this is sometimes, or even often, the case. But to say that it is *always* the case is overstatement. Bereavement is not always a question of being surprised by impermanence. For example, in the case of my mother, who died recently from Alzheimer's, I did not personally find it so. With an Alzheimer's patient, one is more likely to take comfort from the fact that the semi-human state reached by an old person is impermanent, and greet their death as a relief.

In practice, though, what actually proves insightful about the doctrine of impermanence is that quite often people do seem to have an assumption of something being permanent when it is not. For example, people are disappointed when childhood haunts have changed, or fail to take into account the effect of ageing on their marriage. Once more, the doctrine is much more useful, and accurate, when not taken as an insight into how things actually are, but rather as practical guidance into how we ought to avoid seeing them in certain common circumstances. Buddhists, though, are their own worst enemies in presenting a confusing version of their doctrine that claims much more than it practically needs to. It is not the case that all conditioned existence is impermanent, only that we *may* suffer if we are attached to a permanent idea of something that is impermanent.

As with the doctrine of dukkha, one could also just as easily turn this around the other way. What if, instead of a doctrine of impermanence, we had a doctrine of permanence? We think things are constantly changing, and we suffer when they don't but actually stay the same. For example, this would fit the experience of frustration of those trying to make progressive reforms in an atmosphere of stifling conservative bureaucracy. The doctrine of permanence, again, would not be essentially more or less true than the doctrine of impermanence.

Again, it would be true to some experience, but misleading when dogmatically applied as a metaphysical claim about all experience.

Anatta

Finally, there is anatta, often poorly translated as "not-self", but better rendered as "insubstantiality", or even "lack of ultimate substantiality". Anatta basically points out that when we believe there is a definite object, or a definite self, corresponding to a certain label, then we are mistaken. For example, the "chair" I believe I am sitting on is just a convenient way of referring to a set of processes and experiences, but it is my mind that has imposed on it the idea of a "chair" as a defined unchanging object with clear boundaries. Similarly with myself, I tend to believe that there is a fixed thing I call me, when what I actually experience is a set of changing mental and physical states to which I attach that label. Such labels are part of the process of attachment, as I can only be attached to (or reject) something I have thus conceptually parcelled up.

There are strong philosophical arguments that support this basic insight in the Buddhist tradition. The labelling of either an object or a self will vary in different circumstances, given different cultures, languages, and individual experiences. For example, a person from a culture that had never encountered Western technology would not see a computer as an identifiable object as we would. A piece of polystyrene could be a toy for a child, non-biodegradable rubbish for another person, packaging for a warehouse-man, or potential modelling material for someone else. These variations suggest that it is not the object itself, but our way of labelling it, which gives it its identity. Similarly with the boundaries of an object: do I see a car as a set of parts, as an individual object, or part of the traffic? Do I consider my hair and toenails part of me? The boundaries are set by us. When objects or selves start and stop in time also depends on us: when does a foetus become a person? When does grass in the stomach of a rabbit cease to become grass and start to become rabbit?

However, these arguments only support the insight that the labelling of objects comes from our minds, not that there are ultimately no objects. We simply do not know whether there are objects in the world out there, because we only ever perceive them through the filter of our experiences. It makes sense, in some ways, to believe that there are trees and rabbits and boxes and computers, and indeed people. However, if they exist, these things are constantly changing, the labels placed on them may vary, and their boundaries are shifting. Buddhists tend to explain this in terms of objects existing *conventionally* but not *ultimately*[3]. Anatta, then, claims that objects do not ultimately exist, at least in the forms we experience and label them. More philosophically careful Buddhists may also add that anatta means objects do not *not* exist: that is, we do not know ultimately that they do not exist any more than we know that they do exist. All we know is that our conceptions of them are likely to be limited and mistaken.

Once again, then, we have what first appeared to be a metaphysical claim, about objects existing or not existing, but on closer examination the doctrine of anatta (unless crudely expressed or misinterpreted) makes no such claims. It only requires us to bear in mind the limitations of our knowledge. It is intended to leave us in a state of open-minded doubt about objects around us, not a dogmatic assumption that they do not exist. This doctrine becomes of great practical value when it reminds one to reconsider the conceptions that have become the focus of a strong emotional response, such as hatred. I may be carrying round and constantly

---

[3] As in the "two truths" philosophy of Nagarjuna (e.g. for an introduction see Paul Williams <u>Mahayana Buddhism</u> [Routledge 1989] p.69)

reviewing a mental image of the person I hate as having a certain character that led them to do or say certain things against me. However, a re-examination of this idea in the light of anatta might lead me to reflect that they also probably have many other more positive characteristics unknown to me, and it is an idea that I hate rather than a person.

If we separate it from a metaphysical claim, anatta becomes inseparable from the Middle Way. If the Middle Way is a principle of judgement which involves avoiding the dogmatic extremes of eternalism and nihilism, anatta just gives us a further reminder of the limitations of any of these dogmatic views.

Where anatta can be interpreted unhelpfully is where it is seen just as an insight of the state of enlightenment, which is then at such a distance from our experience that we fall back on purely conventional categories. If anatta makes no difference to our lives now, we are not taking its insights seriously enough. If we use it as a reminder of the limitations of our understanding of reality, we can use it to reflect on anything in our experience, and make gradual adjustments so as to make our understanding of that thing better by questioning what we have previously assumed about it.

There is a strong tendency in the Buddhist tradition, however, not to use anatta to question common assumptions at all, but rather just as a way of idealising enlightened experience, which allegedly sees things as they really are beyond concepts. We may reflect that we do not understand things as they really are, but, instead of then investigating them for ourselves, then take this as a reason for depending on an enlightened person's account of them. This approach can often have the effect just of reinforcing a new conventional view, which has grown up around a tradition of what may once have been one (allegedly enlightened) person's insight. Rather than being a tool to gradually rid us of illusions, anatta then shuts us into them more firmly. This, of course, raises many questions about enlightenment and authority in Buddhism, which we will return to later (in the next chapter).

The three lakshanas in general

For dukkha, anicca, and anatta, then, we have found a common pattern. All are based on insights that can be of practical value. However, all three doctrines are commonly presented as metaphysical beliefs, rather than as principles of judgement in relation to our own experience. The presentation of the three lakshanas as metaphysical beliefs is responsible for a great deal of misunderstanding of Buddhism by both Buddhists and non-Buddhists. Those who see Buddhism as a negative and pessimistic religion are not always wrong, as pessimism is a type of dogmatism (insisting inflexibly that things are always worse than experience gives us grounds to believe), and such dogmatism is often encouraged by the way Buddhists present these doctrines. On the other hand, the need to avoid denying the hollowness or lack of satisfaction we often experience, the need to appreciate the impermanence of things we are attached to, and the need to appreciate the way in which we impose categories on our experience are all vital starting points for the spiritual life.

Greed and hatred

The driving forces of conditioned existence are traditionally represented in the centre of the Wheel of Samsara (the diagrammatic representation of the endless cycle in which Buddhism claims we are caught) as three animals: the cock, the snake and the pig, representing greed, hatred and ignorance respectively. Of these, ignorance works together with greed, as we can only have greed for something that we are also under an illusion about, representing it in the way that suits us rather than getting to grips with its more complex and shifting reality. Hatred is seen as frustrated greed, for those we hate are those who prevent us getting what we want. These three forces together create the basis of the Second Noble Truth, traditionally providing an explanation as to why the world we experience is unsatisfactory. Once greed has arisen, we grasp for the object of our greed, thus setting up further conditions for ignorance in the future.

What exactly counts as greed? The Buddhist term translates the Pali word *tanha*, literally "thirst", and sometimes also translated as "craving". We are told by the Buddhist tradition that not all desires are greed or hatred: there is also good desire or *dhamma-chanda*, the desire for enlightenment. Nevertheless, greed covers quite a wide range of desires, from the desire to own a new Mercedes-Benz through to the very desire to continue to exist.

The insight that many people will readily recognise here is that greed does, indeed, cause a great deal of suffering. It narrows our mental states and impairs our judgements, making us obsessed with short-term objectives and leading us to neglect the bigger picture. Greed leads to conflict, corruption, environmental degradation, and neglect. Almost any problem in the world today can be traced to greed (or its frustrated version, hatred) in the mental states of the human beings involved.

So far, Buddhism appears to have struck an important truth. However, there will also have been many thinking Westerners who will have paused to wonder when first introduced to Buddhism, about the beliefs found in Buddhism that our lives themselves are a result of greed, that if we manage to purify ourselves of that greed we reach the ideal state of enlightenment, and that the ceasing of even a greed for life itself is morally and spiritually desirable. At that point they may have turned away from Buddhism, concluding that it is a "life-denying" religion. Alternatively, they may have carried on, choosing to set aside their unease because of experience that in practice Buddhism is often far from life-denying, but rather offers practices that greatly enhance life.

Many Buddhist practices have also arisen out of the experience of practitioners who recognise that "purifying" ourselves of greed is a hopeless project. Instead they focus on following the Middle Way by *transforming* greed into more useful or subtle forms. For example, the energy given to the fruitless pursuit of the ideal house or the ideal partner could be much better channelled into developing one's own awareness or into supporting others. The hatred put into fruitless rivalries with work colleagues could also be transformed into wisdom that seeks the truth. However, in transforming ourselves in this way we are not purifying ourselves of greed, but rather focusing it on more useful objects, and perhaps also gaining a closer control over it.

The practices of Buddhism are well developed, and offer many useful methods of transformation, but the theory also seems to be deeply confused and is not fully devoted to supporting this practice. Not only is the language of purification frequently used (especially in Buddhist ritual) rather than the language of transformation, but the very symbol of everything that Buddhists are working for, the Buddha, represents an enlightened person who has purified themselves of all greed, up to and including even the desire for life itself.

The interpretation of the ideal of enlightenment is a big and complex issue that we will have to return to from many different angles. However, let's simply stick to the point at the moment that the ideal represented by Buddhists is of a person without any greed whatsoever.

There seem to be several unnecessary assumptions in traditional Buddhist thinking here. One of these is that because many problems causing suffering or dissatisfaction have greed as one of their necessary elements, these problems can be solved by removing the greed. On the contrary, if we remove the greed, it may be that many positives are removed along with negatives. If we remove sexual desire, for example, not only are the problems caused by sexual desire removed (such as abusive or neurotic relationships, and overpopulation), but also the psychological fulfilments we gain through sexual activity, or from its consequences in the shape of committed sexual relationships and children.

Buddhists are often remarkably straightforward about sex, and Buddhist practice often attempts to be realistic in addressing the conditions created by sexual desire in our physical and psychological constitutions. Yet nevertheless, the *ideal* that is the symbolic, ritual and doctrinal focus of Buddhism is not one of transforming sexual energy positively and avoiding its unskilful use: instead, it is one of being entirely free of sexual desire. The ideal is constantly at odds with balanced, skilful practice.

Another unnecessary assumption made in traditional Buddhist thinking is that the weakening and/or transformation of greed, if carried on for long enough, necessarily leads to its complete disappearance. However, that it is good to reduce something does not necessarily mean that it is good to get rid of it altogether. This is something that every sane slimmer knows. There is a point where to lose further weight is to move beyond the point of balance and health and to enter the realm of obsessive anorexia. Perhaps it is good to reduce our level of greed by transforming it into skilful forms of desire, but it no more follows this that we should seek to extinguish greed than that a slimmer should try to starve themselves to death in pursuit of an idealised state of "health".

It may be objected here that this point is already recognised in Buddhism in the distinction between greed (*tanha*) and desire for enlightenment (*dhamma-chanda*). The enlightened ideal, it might be said, is not to be free of all desires, but rather to only have desires that are completely objective, disinterested, and free of self-view. This ideal might be claimed to be transformational rather than purificatory, for the energy that we invest in greed simply needs to be transformed into a desire for enlightenment. However, this way of thinking about the Buddhist ideal apparently fails to recognise the ways that greed (rather than any other form of desire) seems to be an ineradicable part of our nature. We may be able to transform it to some extent, but that does not mean we can transform it completely. In some cases we may even manage a well-regulated state of celibacy, but we are still sexual beings. We may manage to avoid gluttony and neuroticism about food, but enjoyment of food will still be a very basic part of our being. We may have come to terms with the inevitability of death, yet we still desire to remain alive. If a Buddha is actually meant to be a person who has maximally transformed his greed, having only the ineradicable elements left, rather than someone completely without greed, the traditional depictions certainly often fail to present him in that way.

For the fact of the matter is that we are human, and that Buddhism has long ago abandoned the Middle Way when it has departed from a positive acceptance of that human state. We are beings full of lusts and appetites, and these are part of what makes us human in the first place. If the Buddhist account of what it is to be human is that we are saddled with greed of a kind that we really *should* get rid of even though we in fact cannot, then Buddhism offers no improvement on the belief in Original Sin found in traditional Christianity (which many Western Buddhists from Christian backgrounds started off by rejecting). We have no more practical chance of shaking off greed completely than of shaking off original sin completely.

The mistake made by traditional Buddhism is to accept a metaphysical view of unenlightened human nature as directed by greed, and enlightened human nature as entirely free of it. Like all metaphysical beliefs, this dogmatically over-simplifies the complex causal relationships we encounter in experience. This metaphysical belief is also in conflict with the practical benefits of Buddhist practice, which begin with our practical experience of being a human being with appetites and lusts. Buddhist practice should consistently be helping us to work with that experience, rather than subtly undermining our acceptance of it through contradictory ideals.

Everything that has been said here about greed can also be applied, *mutatis mutandis*, to hatred. As the Buddhist tradition recognises, hatred can be transformed into wisdom. However, it also seems likely from common human experience that we are stuck with some degree of hatred. We can turn our hatred towards things that are actually harmful rather than towards people that we merely project "evil" onto, and we can express our hatred only in controlled and appropriate ways, but common human experience does not suggest that hatred can be erased, at least without erasing much that is positive too. We seem unavoidably in rivalry not only with other human beings, but also with other forms of life, and such rivalry has many positive evolutionary functions in stimulating adaptation and effort that would not otherwise take place.

Were it not for some degree of hatred, I am sure, I would not be writing this book. However, my "hatred" of some aspects of traditional Buddhism seems to be controlled, balanced and subject to reflection. It is much less obviously negative in its likely effects than a gross unreflective hatred. The idea that a critique such as this should not be undertaken because it may be motivated by such controlled hatreds is based on assumptions of a kind that I cannot accept.

The possibility of progress

The Third Noble Truth is traditionally stated as the truth of Nirvana, or in Pali *Nibbana*. That is, that enlightenment is possible as an alternative to the cycle of unenlightened existence, and that we can get beyond greed, hatred, ignorance, and the dukkha that results from them, into a state of endless calm and wisdom.

Once this possibility has been asserted (usually by the historical assertion that the Buddha actually attained this state), the Path, or Fourth Noble Truth, is then traditionally asserted. If there is an alternative to the unenlightened cycle, the Path can then be understood as the way to move from the unenlightened state to the enlightened state. Before we set out on the Path, it is assumed, we need to know where we are going.

Except that, at the same time, it is admitted that we do not know where we are going. Buddhist assertions about the metaphysical status of nirvana are nearly always accompanied by further assertions of how little we know about it, and how difficult it is to understand from the unenlightened perspective. The odd thing is that this acknowledgement of ignorance never extends to questioning whether we need the conception at all, let alone whether Buddhists need to believe in it. Buddhists are usually prepared to accept a vague open-mindedness about nirvana, but in my experience, they are not usually prepared to address the unnecessary assumptions on which Buddhist belief in it is based.

The first of these unnecessary assumptions is the underlying idea that a Path necessarily needs a goal. Of course, if we set out on a journey, having some idea where we are going is often a good practical motivator. However, if the journey is understood as an especially long and mysterious one, there is no requirement at all for an ultimate destination to even be named, let alone known in any detail. When I reach a fork in the road, I will probably need a reason for choosing one route rather than another in the form of an *intermediate* goal. However, having an ultimate goal (especially when it is not always clear what the best route is to that ultimate goal) is more likely to confuse me than otherwise.

To switch the metaphor, it is also not always good to plan too far ahead. A teenager making precise plans for her retirement would not only be an oddity: she would also be wasting her energy, for many of the assumed conditions on which the planning would have to be based would be too much subject to change during the intervening time. A Buddhist who says that they are aiming for nirvana (whether in this lifetime or a later one) and claims to find this a meaningful and genuinely encouraging goal, does not in fact (on their own admission) know what they are talking about, and is almost inevitably applying the label "nirvana" to some lesser intermediate goal. When Buddhists claim to recognise that they do not know what nirvana is, but also still use the concept to represent a goal, they not only do not know what they are talking about, but they are contradicting themselves.

As with the other Noble Truths, however, there is nevertheless an insight behind the contradictions. What nirvana does genuinely seem to represent for many Buddhists is the mere possibility of progress. We would not be motivated to move outside our current comfort zone, or to make any effort in spiritual practice, if we did not believe that progress was possible. What "nirvana" can mean, for many Buddhists, is the realisation "Yes, I can move beyond this self-destructive cycle of unreflective craving or hatred. Yes, I can break this addiction or this bad habit, however deeply entrenched it seems to be. Yes, I can be different from what I am now."

Clearly such realisations can be of tremendous positive importance for all of us.

A further unnecessary assumption commonly made in Buddhism, then, is that the possibility of progress is based on nirvana. That nirvana must have existed as a state achieved by the Buddha, and perhaps by other Buddhist teachers, and that believing in the past achievement of this state somehow makes progress in our current situation more possible.

On the contrary, the reality or non-reality of this historical event is of no relevance at all to the possibility of us making progress. Someone known to us who makes progress in a way we can understand and relate to may have a strong effect, but it is this assurance of progress in particular cases in our experience that encourages us, not the assurance of progress in general drawn from the abstraction of an unattainable goal apparently gained thousands of years ago. Again, perhaps Buddhists often use the enlightenment of the Buddha to stand for or symbolise more specific goals that relate to their experience, but in that case, it is the specific achievable goals that make the Buddha's enlightenment meaningful, not the other way round.

Worse, the assurance of this past event takes place in such abstraction that it frequently becomes the basis of dogmatic beliefs about the authority of the Buddha's teachings. This is an issue I shall return to in the next chapter. In this case, belief in the Buddha's enlightenment is not just irrelevant to progress, but it has the negative effect of passing off our own responsibility for our progress onto the authority of a past enlightened master, and leading us to take his words far too seriously.

So, the insight that lies behind the Third Noble Truth seems to be that of the possibility of moral and spiritual progress, a possibility which must first be experienced. That experience might then be symbolised by the enlightenment of the Buddha (as it might by many other things), but it is a major error to think that there is any necessary link or requirement between spiritual progress and belief that the Buddha was enlightened.

A third unnecessary assumption made in traditional Buddhism seems to be that the Third Noble Truth logically precedes the Fourth one, i.e. that the Path must be defined (and indeed can only be understood at all) in terms of its ultimate goal. On the contrary, the Third Noble Truth can only be understood in terms of the Fourth: we only begin to recognise where we are going when we set out on the journey.

We cannot possibly claim to know any truths of the universe without first having a method for getting near to discovering them. The Fourth Noble Truth, in the shape of the Middle Way, provides a general principle as to what kind of method should be successful in getting to grips with conditions. Anything we know about the possibility of progress depends on that principle and its application, as we experiment to find out what produces progress and what does not. We cannot start with the possibility of progress and then derive a method of gaining it from that possibility, because the mere possibility of progress tells us nothing concrete about how to make progress.

Again, the defect in the traditional Buddhist approach here is that it is metaphysical. It starts off by claiming to know truths about the universe and then derives further "truths" from this. Instead, I am recommending an *epistemological* approach, i.e. one that starts with the question of how we justify our beliefs.

The four noble principles

So, it should be becoming clearer by now that, although there are important insights to be found in the Buddhist teaching of the Four Noble Truths, they are not "truths" at all. What they offer of value is instead principles of approach. To avoid confusions and contradictions, to be in harmony with the Middle Way, and to give appropriate support to Buddhist practices, I suggest that they be not only re-phrased but also re-ordered. The results might be something like this:
1. The First Noble Principle: The Middle Way is the Principle of investigation which allows us to get closer to truth through experience
2. The Second Noble Principle: If we are to improve the problematic and unsatisfactory aspects of our experience, we must first recognise that they are problematic and unsatisfactory.
3. The Third Noble Principle: Aspects of our experience are often made problematic and unsatisfactory by greed of a type that can be transformed and rechannelled.
4. The Fourth Noble Principle: Investigating our experience usually shows that progress is possible.

Chapter 2: The sources of justified belief in Buddhism

The confusing of sources of knowledge in Buddhism

In the first chapter there were some major assumptions about how we justify our beliefs. How do we know that we are going about things in the right way? Before we go any further in considering the doctrines of Buddhism, it is important to clarify this. To do so will also be part of my case that Buddhism has often betrayed its own core insights, for the assumptions that it has made about how we know are at the base of this betrayal.

How do we know anything? Philosophy suggests three possible ways: experience (of many different kinds), reason, and revelation. Of these, reason largely only processes the other two and assesses them for consistency. Reason does not give us new information, except (debatably) mathematical or logical information. There has been a lengthy debate about the role of reason in Western philosophy, but this need not concern us much here. It is experience and revelation that have been of the most concern to Buddhists.

On the face of it, Buddhism is unique among religions in the amount of emphasis it gives to experience as a source of knowledge. In the often-quoted *Kalama Sutta*[4], the Buddha responds to a group of confused villagers who have listened to too many conflicting claims from different religious leaders. They ask the Buddha whom they should believe, and how they can know who is right. The Buddha responds that they should not simply accept what is claimed on the authority of the person saying it, or because it is traditional or in a scripture. Instead, he says "When you yourselves know" the policy of the wise, then you should follow it.

This is often interpreted to mean that our own experience should be the measure of the truth. Exactly how this is interpreted, however, does vary. More conservative Buddhists[5] will point to the reference to the wise and claim that, once we know who is

---

[4] Anguttara Nikaya 3.65. For an online translation see http://www.accesstoinsight.org/tipitaka/an/an03/an03.065.than.html

[5] E.g. see Bhikkhu Bodhi's essay 'A Look at the Kalama Sutta', http://www.accesstoinsight.org/lib/authors/bodhi/bps-essay_09.html

wise and have committed ourselves to following them, it is their guidance that is important. They also point out that the Buddha was speaking to uncommitted villagers, not committed followers of the Buddha. We may have no choice but to consult our own experience when we remain in doubt about whom to follow, but the conservative Buddhist case seems to be that it is not trustworthy in the long run. If our own experience told us all we needed to know, after all, why follow the Buddha at all?

So, the Kalama Sutta is ambiguous as evidence that experience is of prime importance in Buddhism. It is also in competition with a strong tradition of appealing to the Buddha's enlightenment as a source of truth. The Buddha's enlightenment, if it happened as it is told, was an experience of the Buddha. It is also claimed that we ourselves can reproduce this experience. However, we are not enlightened now, so we do not experience enlightenment but rather the illusions of unenlightened existence. So, at least in the earlier forms of Buddhism, there is an appeal to experience in the abstract, but not an appeal to *our* experience *now*, or even in the foreseeable or probable future.

Instead, the reliance is on the Buddha's experience of enlightenment as a source of truth. This appeal to the Buddha's experience I would describe as *revelation*, because that is how it appears to us now. The truth is claimed to have been revealed to us by the Buddha, whose words are then enshrined in Buddhist scriptures. The Buddha, it is claimed, had access to a level of truth that we do not currently have, and for that reason we should follow his advice.

Some Buddhists object to the use of the term revelation, which they associate with monotheistic religions such as Christianity and Islam. If pressed to define what they understand revelation to be, they would probably say that it must come from God. However, the word of the Buddha in traditional Buddhism functions in a very similar way to the way that the word of God functions in Christianity or Islam. The source of knowledge is far beyond what we can access ourselves, and it makes claims to perfection and finality that are very similar to those made for divine revelation. The ultimate source of the claimed truth (God vs. Buddha) is much less important than the claimed authority that is given to it. In both cases, in practice, that authority places the claims ascribed to it far beyond examination through experience.

So, if Buddhists claim that their religion is based on experience, and yet claim to be followers of the Buddha and to accept his words as authoritative, they are contradicting themselves. Just because Buddhists do not appeal to God, this does not mean their religion is not one based on revelation, nor that they don't have to deal with the issues that revelation brings with it. It is not God that is the issue here, but rather our lack of access to the validating experience that supposedly tells us the truth about the state of enlightenment. Without access to this validation, we cannot have any justification for believing that the Buddha's claims are true, but merely have faith in them, just as monotheistic believers have faith in God.

Nor is validation of the truth of the Buddha's words any nearer for Buddhists than it is for Christians or Muslims. Buddhists may protest that they themselves may in future attain enlightenment and thus gain access to a perfect validation, but those who believe in God may also have a religious experience in which God will make his will indubitably clear. At the end of history God may make everything clear to everyone, but this is scarcely any less close to our experience, or any less predictable, than when we will ourselves gain a state of perfect enlightenment. In either case, faith is justified by the appeal to more faith that this will in fact occur.

Other Buddhists (particularly Mahayana Buddhists) are likely to say here that a distant enlightenment is not actually the basis of knowledge in Buddhism. Instead, we should recognise that we are enlightened already, and simply consult our experience in the present. Our intuitive experience, they will say, tells us that the Buddha's teachings are correct. Others may lay the emphasis on a gradual or provisional engagement with the Buddha's advice.

In either case here, there is one important question to be asked to determine whether experience is really the basis of judgement for these Buddhists, or whether they are just paying lip service to it. Do they follow the Buddha's teachings because they are the Buddha's teachings, or because they just appear to be useful? If they respond that usefulness is their criterion, then the Buddha's teachings should be given no more priority than any other useful teachings. The source of the advice should be irrelevant.

Of course, practically speaking, the source of advice that we follow is rarely irrelevant. We build up relationships of trust with people, and if we find them to be reliable, we are likely to follow their advice in the future. For example, if I take my bicycle for a service and the mechanic, whom I have been using to service my bike for years, tells me that the bike needs a new bottom bracket. I am liable to simply believe him, rather than taking the bike round several other shops to get different opinions, or researching the subject in any other way. Can the relationship with the Buddha not be a similarly practical one of trust based on experience?

This might be the basis of judgement about real people whom we know, including Buddhist teachers that we know personally. However, it can hardly be the basis of judgement about a man who lived 2500 years ago, whose personality is mediated by ancient scriptures and traditions. To trust a "Buddha" based on these is actually to trust tradition or to trust scripture, neither of which is in itself trustworthy (a point we will return to later in this chapter). To appeal to a Buddha based on these is not to justify a personal trust through our own previous experience, but again simply to adopt an attitude of faith.

None of this stops the Buddha's advice being good advice. But then, Jesus' advice may also be good advice. Marx's advice may be good advice. My local bicycle mechanic's advice may be good advice. The basis on which I judge whether to trust it can only be my own experience, not the source of the advice regardless of my experience. This then implies that Buddhists who really believe that the basis of their religion is experience should investigate other sources of good advice with impartiality, rather than relying solely on the Buddha, or expecting that the Buddha's advice will always take priority over other sources. If they do give the Buddha's advice priority, it should be acknowledged that this approach is based on faith or commitment to tradition, not experience.

So, probably the first step for many Buddhists is one of greater honesty and transparency in their understanding of what their sources of belief actually are, and how they justify their faith in Buddhism. To use "experience" as a bland or vague term to cover the source of knowledge in Buddhism, when they are actually believers in a revelation, is both misleading and disingenuous.

Once Buddhists are clear about what they believe the sources of knowledge actually are, they are in a better position to consider whether these sources are justified. My argument in the remainder of this chapter will be that to use revelation as a source of knowledge at all is to betray the central insights of Buddhism, and that experience should be our sole source of justified belief. To see why this should be the case we need to look again at the Middle Way.

Justified beliefs from the Middle Way

One of the major insights of the Buddhist tradition is that our experience (or our interpretation of experience) is often distorted by greed, hatred and ignorance. The version of events on which we judge our actions is often created by wishful thinking rather than the fullest attempt to uncover the truth of the matter. We make ourselves believe in someone's virtues because we desire them, or we go to war in Iraq in the belief that this will contribute to reducing terrorism. We can even delude ourselves that we are following higher spiritual teachings whilst following the basest of motives. Our experience, it seems, is not to be trusted to let us know what is true or what is good.

Yet we also have no alternative. We are trapped within our own experience, and everything is mediated through it. We cannot simply escape from our own skins into some sudden godlike eminence, where we know the truth for sure. Even if it is true that there are or have been enlightened beings who have got beyond all greed, hatred and ignorance (let us grant it for now, though this may well be a fantasy too), we cannot avoid interpreting what they say or do through our own unenlightened experience. Whatever we believe, the justification for it will have to come through our own flawed experience, because that's all we've got that does not involve the delusion of some leap beyond it.

However, there is a way forward in this situation that does not involve either the deluded god-fantasy or, on the other hand, a slide into relativism where no justified belief is possible and there are only many jostling opinions as good as each other. This way forward is offered by the Middle Way, which provides us with a way of testing the conclusions of experience for objectivity. Science may be helpful in pursuing the Middle Way, but the Middle Way goes much further than science, encompassing objectivity in relation to our internal experiences, and objectivity in moral and spiritual judgements, not just objectivity in relation to publicly observable factual claims.

The Middle Way allows us to become more objective because it consists in the avoidance of both eternalist metaphysics on the one hand and nihilist metaphysics on the other. It alerts us to the kinds of dogmatic assumptions we might make that will trap us in illusion, and thus enables us to cast off burdens of falsehood, even if we are never sure of having reached complete truth. What we do know is that experience does not offer either positive or negative certainties. We cannot ever say either that we have reached the complete truth, or that there is no truth. Instead, we can work with the information that experience provides us with to get ever closer to the truth.

We do this, however, not by developing a final verbal account of it, such as a revelation or a scientific law, but by becoming gradually more objective as people. Objectivity as offered by the Middle Way is *dispositional* (based on the tendencies of people) and *incremental* (involving gradual change, never reaching an absolute point). It does not give us a verbal description of the absolute truth, but it provides two rocks of falsehood between which to navigate, eternalism and nihilism. Broadly speaking, eternalism involves the positive assertion of absolute metaphysical claims, whilst nihilism involves their equally absolute denial.

At the time of the Buddha, the predominant positive and negative metaphysical claims which people tended to become attached to were those concerning the presence or absence of the self. Belief in the existence of an absolute and permanent self or soul, which existed unchanging through an infinite series of lives, was linked in early Hindu thought with belief in the moral laws of the universe, which provided the standard according to which the self could be judged. A meritorious life where moral credit had been earned would result in improved status in one's next reincarnation, but on the other hand bad deeds would result in moral debits and a worse position in future lives. This was the eternalism of the Buddha's day, which formed the basis of moral order in society.

The nihilism of the Buddha's day consisted in a denial of this: the belief that there was no permanent self, and thus no continuity between one life and the next. Without this there was no basis of judgement of right and wrong, and thus the complete denial of the permanent self was associated with the denial of all moral values.

The major mistake made by traditional Buddhism in interpreting the Middle Way is to identify eternalism and nihilism with their specific manifestations in the time of the Buddha, rather than generalising to the more universal insight that underlies it. Thus, many Buddhists will simply tell you that eternalism consists in the belief in the eternal self, and nihilism (or annihilationism) consists in denial of the eternal self. If you take this narrow and limited approach, the Middle Way simply becomes a belief in the effects of actions continuing into future lives as a personal causal link rather than as an unchanging self, (the issues of rebirth that this raises will be explored more in chapter 4). The Middle Way thus betrayed becomes merely an irrelevant piece of metaphysics rather than the practical solution to the problems of philosophy that it potentially offers.

For who cares about the permanent existence of the self in the West today? Nobody is better or worse because of believing in it or not. Believing in it may possibly have been the basis of the moral order in the Indian society of the Buddha's time, but it can hardly be said to be the basis of any moral motivation today. Not even the traditional Christian equivalent, the threat of heaven or hell following the judgement of God, any longer inspires more than a small minority to moral belief. Nor, on the other hand, does disbelief in it have either a particularly moral effect or a particularly immoral effect. Reincarnation, rebirth, and the soul are simply moral and spiritual irrelevancies, the concern only of a few speculative theologians. Thus a bunch of people wandering into the Western context claiming that the Middle Way between believing in future lives and not believing in them is somehow the basis of all our salvations are deservedly ignored. Presented in this way, it is not surprising if even many Buddhists just find the Middle Way irrelevant and forget about it.

No, the eternalism and nihilism of today are found in the types of metaphysics that people are actually attached to and care about: for example the saving power of Jesus, the "Pro-life" convictions, the Fundamentalist belief in the word of the Bible or of the Qur'an, the belief that following "nature" will cure our ills; or on the other hand, consumerism, youth culture, conventional values, and hedonistic excess, all of which place immediate beliefs or desires before any higher or more objective beliefs. There are other kinds of moral absolutes in currency today, and other ways of denying them. If Buddhism is to be relevant, its account of the Middle Way needs to encompass these.

However, the Middle Way should also not be too strongly identified with the "sensible" conventional middle ground of opinion. If society is heavily influenced by metaphysical assumptions, then the Middle Way can be quite radical in challenging them. If major aspects of people's moral behaviour are hugely adrift from facing up to conditions (as is the case in many Western people's attitude to eating meat and dairy products, for example) then the Middle Way may be quite radical in urging an objective need to address those conditions. Radical changes can result from applying it, even if the need to address psychological conditions still forms a part of the picture. It is not easy to change people's habits, and much easier to delude ourselves that we have changed when we have not. The Middle Way always demands real change rather than short-lived fake change, but the demands may still be radical for all that, and despite the name there is nothing essentially moderate about it.

So, however much it may have been neglected or misunderstood by Buddhists, the Middle Way does offer a way of justifying our beliefs. Such justification is based on experience of all kinds, examined through reason. If we avoid the dogmatic extremes offered by metaphysics, we are at least equipped for engaging with the truth. The justified beliefs it yields will never be absolute, but they can be objective, moving beyond our previous limiting assumptions. It offers us a far more reliable approach to justifying our beliefs than any supposed revelation, for there are no short cuts to the truth, only a long slow process of peeling away delusion.

The trouble with Buddhist metaphysics

However, the above argument is likely to leave other questions. What exactly counts as metaphysics? Is it really possible to separate metaphysics from claims about what can be experienced? Is Buddhist metaphysics not different from other metaphysics?

These kinds of issues have really not been clarified by the Buddhist tradition. The Buddha gave four metaphysical topics that he said it would not be helpful to give answers about: the end of the universe, the end of time, the existence of the self or soul, and the continued existence of the Buddha after death[6]. As with the Buddha's teachings on the Middle Way, the way to make these teachings useful in contexts other than the Buddha's is to interpret them as examples, and work out the general principle which makes a topic metaphysical and thus not useful to speculate about, which could be applied to other examples. However, the Buddhist tradition has not done this. Instead, it has largely limited its discussion to these particular examples, which reflect the metaphysical concerns of the Buddha's time rather than ours. It has also succeeded in removing a lot of the power and insight from the Buddha's teaching on this point by claiming that the Buddha did in fact know the answers to these questions, but that he did not consider his disciples ready to understand the answers[7].

If it is interpreted as just a piece of esotericism, then the Buddhist tradition has completely misunderstood the insight that can be gained from the Buddha's teaching here. It is not that there are metaphysical

---

[6] This formula, often known as the *avyakrta* or 'Silence of the Buddha', is found at several points in the Pali Canon. One of the best-known is the *Culamalunkya Sutta* (Majjhima Nikaya 63)

[7] The idea that the Buddha actually knew about an unconditioned reality is often supported by the passage in the *Udana* (section 8) quoted below in chapter 6: "There is, monks, an unborn, unbecome…"

truths, but they can only be known by the enlightened and cannot be expressed in words. If you believe this, then you have no access to the truth from an unenlightened state, and you are inevitably led back into dependence on revelation from the Buddha, and thus abandonment of the Middle Way. The Buddha's point is much more profound than this: there *are* no metaphysical truths. If "truth" takes a metaphysical form then you are just barking up the wrong tree. If the enlightened have grasped anything, it is that truth lies beyond metaphysics.

Take the example of the beginning or the end of time. There is no "answer" to the question as to when the universe began, because any possible answer will still raise the further question "What happened before then?". The Big Bang Theory may well be correct, but it is not about the beginning of the universe. Physicists simply do not know (though they may speculate) what happened before the Big Bang. Even if further theories about what happened before the Big Bang turn out to be supportable with evidence in the future, we will still always be able to ask what happened before that. The question is fruitless because we know when we start asking it that we can never possibly find an answer. It is necessarily true that all answers to this question will be speculative and the pursuit of it will be a waste of time.

What makes it a waste of time is the lack of relationship of any possible answer to the question to any possible experience. Without such a relationship, not only are answers going to be speculative, but also any such answers (even if they happen, by chance, to be correct) have no further moral or spiritual relationship to our practical experience. Christians may claim, for example, that because God made the universe, everything in the universe is essentially good. However, neither "God" nor "essentially good" have any purchase on our experience. Whatever happens, even if the whole universe was a hell of endless suffering, it would not be incompatible with it being *essentially* good, for what is essentially good does not have to be good in our experience. Any possible experience is compatible with the claim that God exists and created a good universe, or that he didn't. Explaining away the apparent counter-examples, such as Auschwitz or toothache, is child's play to a practised theologian. So, whether God exists and created the universe and whether it is essentially good or not, we are under no new moral obligations compared to the ones we had before, since moral obligations can only be found in experience. Similarly, God's existence or non-existence yields no new spiritual insights, because these too need to be experienced.

Christian dogmas can easily be identified as metaphysical, but even those who readily acknowledge the uselessness of such dogma may still defend other types of metaphysics. For example, it may be claimed that some scientific theories are metaphysical, because they can never be conclusively proved in their own right, even though they imply other theories that can. Nevertheless, these "metaphysical" scientific theories have practical implications, and thus are not subject to the same criticisms as dogmatic metaphysics. We cannot prove through observation, for example, whether electrons exist or not. However, theories involving electrons have explanatory value, and are consistent with other theories that do relate to experience – hence they are not metaphysical. The same is true of the theory of the Middle Way itself, which cannot be directly proved, but only applied and proved fruitful indirectly.

It may also be the case that the boundaries of metaphysics are fuzzy. With some sorts of claims, it may be doubtful whether or not they are metaphysical: however, the fuzziness of boundaries should not stop us using the term "metaphysics" any more than it should stop us using any other useful concept. It may not be clear, as the suburbs gradually peter out, where the town ends and the countryside begins, but this does not stop us usefully using the terms "town" and "countryside". Nor does the concept of metaphysics require non-metaphysical claims to be conclusively provable through experience: the point is that metaphysical claims are clearly neither verifiable nor falsifiable, and that their promotion involves avoidance of the healthy uncertainty surrounding every other kind of claim.

If we take the Buddha's metaphysical questions merely as examples from his own time, there are many other kinds of claims in our own time that are clearly metaphysical. They are the basis of endless, fruitless argument, both by philosophers and by ordinary people. The answers to the questions could not possibly make any difference to anyone's life, because any answer is consistent with any experience or the justification of any action. However, people nevertheless believe these claims to be the essential basis of their beliefs. Some of the important ones of our time are as follows

- whether there is only material substance (materialism vs dualism)

- whether God exists
- whether there is freewill or determinism
- whether there is an ultimate source of good
- whether there is a real world or merely sets of perceptions (realism vs. idealism)
- whether there is an absolute standard of aesthetic judgement or merely differing tastes
- whether sciences dealing with more complex objects can be entirely reduced to those dealing in simpler ones (e.g. whether psychology can be reduced to biology, or biology to chemistry).

The problem with holding beliefs on any of these questions is that they are inevitably dogmatic. The only possible motivation for holding them is not a justification based on experience, but attachment to an idea believed in by a group. Believing in God, for example, will help to gain the approval of the other people in my society who believe in God. I can then be easily manipulated by religious leaders who tell me what God's instructions are. These instructions could be anything – for example killing my only son, going on a Crusade, or defending the interests of the ruling classes – and I would have no way of checking out whether they were really God's instructions or not. If they seem evil, they will be presented as serving a higher good known only to God.

Some positive effects are often attributed to metaphysical beliefs, when it is the practical insights that accompany them that enable those positive effects. For example, was Mother Theresa enabled to care for the dying in Calcutta by her belief in God, or by her practical compassion and awareness of the needs of the people she served? Well, one can imagine an atheist doing what she did practically, but one cannot imagine someone without compassion doing so: it is clearly the compassion that is essential, not the belief. It is when Mother Theresa invoked her metaphysical beliefs directly that her actions became much more morally questionable – for example her opposition to any larger changes in society to prevent the causes of poverty amongst the people she served, because she did not believe it to be the will of God.

Metaphysics is at best a waste of time, but more commonly the source of evil. Having a fixed idea in our minds that is not open to examination, we do deeds that are out of harmony with conditions. In more traditional Buddhist terms, we act on the basis of ignorance. Some metaphysics is explicitly invoked to justify evil, as in the case of Islamist terrorism. Other metaphysics is only lurking in background assumptions and would take much analysis (either philosophical or psychological) to bring out: for example the effects of an assumed metaphysical belief that someone else is not as fully human as you are, or of the belief that the consequences of one's actions are unreal.

If this is the central point offered by the Buddha, then far from being universally recognised by Buddhists, it is at best inconsistently applied and at worst totally ignored. For most of the Buddhist tradition, far from avoiding metaphysics, actively promotes it. "Buddhist metaphysics" is even accepted as a field of study without being considered an oxymoron.

We have already mentioned some of the metaphysical beliefs to be found in Buddhism. The following are strong candidates for the label "metaphysical":
- belief in the possibility of enlightenment
- belief that the progress of Buddhists depends on the historical enlightenment of the Buddha or other past teachers

- belief in bodhisattvas
- belief in karma and rebirth (see chapter 4)
- belief in universal conditionality or *paticcasamuppada* (see chapter 5)
- belief in the "natural" basis of Buddhist ethics
- belief that particular teachers are enlightened or are stream entrants
- belief in the impermanence, insubstantiality and unsatisfactoriness of all conditioned things (see chapter 1).

None of these beliefs, at least when commonly put into a metaphysical form, bear any justification through experience. Whether the Buddha did or did not achieve enlightenment, it is my practical understanding and inspiration that supports my spiritual progression, not this. Similarly, since we cannot even imagine a world that we do not assume to be conditioned, we are in no position to find out through experience whether the world actually is completely conditioned or not (see chapter 5 for more on this issue).

The question of metaphysics is subject to much Buddhist exceptionalism. Buddhists often seem to think that other religions have metaphysics of the type the Buddha criticised, but they do not really, or their metaphysics is different. The Buddha's criticism of metaphysics, in fact, primarily seems to have the function of *preventing* Buddhists from really asking the same questions about their own beliefs as the ones they ask about others. It is assumed that because the Buddha's doctrines contain a criticism of metaphysics then Buddhism cannot possibly be metaphysical. The Buddha's criticism of metaphysics commonly serves as a spoiler for criticisms of Buddhism, or as a diversion, but it is certainly not applied to the central doctrines of the religion or to their interpretation.

Much of the rest of this book is concerned in one way or another with Buddhist metaphysics, and Buddhism's slippage from the Middle Way into eternalism. Each of the areas of metaphysical claims mentioned above will be discussed in more detail, and the metaphysics differentiated from the useful associated ideas. For the moment though, I want to complete this chapter with more discussion of the sources of knowledge commonly used in Buddhism: that is Buddhist teachers and scriptures.

The trouble with gurus

An important part of the entire Buddhist tradition is the high status and authority given to teachers as sources of knowledge. In Tibetan Buddhism, particularly, the guru is venerated and can be an object of devotion in himself, standing in for the Buddha. The Protestant tradition of egalitarianism, the number of guru scare stories surrounding Indian gurus who have abused their power, and the monotheist suspicion of idol worship all perhaps combine to sometimes make Western Buddhists especially defensive about this aspect of their tradition. However, the fact that it may have been misunderstood and that many negative non-Buddhist reactions to it are unreflective are no reason for not making a more balanced critical appraisal of it.

The strength of the guru tradition is the power of the personal. Instead of a distant revelation from a Buddha figure, Tibetan Buddhists are more likely to venerate a living person who, for them, embodies spiritual qualities. This teacher can instruct them in a way that is geared specifically to their needs, and provide a strong model and example in practice. In this way a sense of a person's virtues and trustworthiness can be genuinely based on experience.

However, the role of guru goes beyond that merely of teacher or of role model. The guru is given superior social status, for example by sitting on a throne whilst teaching. Disciples are encouraged to cultivate gratitude to the guru. Traditionally, the guru is given the absolute role of the Buddha, representing the enlightened perspective. The only way the disciple can get out of his/her ignorance is by absolute adherence to the instructions of the guru. The guru is also revered in his absence: his photograph may be put on a shrine, his image may be visualised in meditation and prostrated before, and he may even have his own mantra chanted in his honour.

This goes much further than a relationship of trust built up through experience. Not only may the guru in practice actually be quite a distant figure, revered by the disciple rather than personally known, but this human figure is also given a metaphysical attachment: the absolute revelatory status of the Buddha.

Scare stories about the misdeeds of gurus, particularly financial and sexual, should not really be needed to alert us to the fact that gurus are human and fallible. Nevertheless, disciples who believe that they have found a crucial figure who will help them reach enlightenment are not likely to be in the kind of mood to learn from history. They may say that the figure of the guru simply represents what is highest and best in themselves, and that revering the guru simply helps to bring this out. In order to do this, however, they have to idealise a living, fallible person. There is a subtle line to be crossed somewhere between being inspired by a person whom one knows personally, and worshipping a person whom one either does not know personally, or idealises, or both. The former might help one follow the Middle Way by providing a source of challenging friendship and objective guidance, but the latter is much more likely to lead one away from it, by feeding delusions about the guru and by forestalling any of the critical perspective that is needed to help one develop a more objective response to his words.

Unfortunately Buddhism, particularly Tibetan Buddhism, frequently crosses that subtle line, and explicitly encourages the idealisation of the guru, for example through teaching the practice of *guru yoga*, where a lineage of gurus is visualised. To deliberately idealise the guru and yet not expect any confusion between the idealisation and the flawed person is to overestimate human rationality. If other Buddhist practices aim to positively recondition the human mind, for example into a positive emotional response towards a former enemy, why should a regular practice of idealising a person not condition the mind into an idealised response to them face-to-face?

One does not need a knee-jerk Western egalitarianism, or an irrational Protestant fear of idol worship, to disapprove of the guru tradition as it has developed in Buddhism. As often, here, the Buddhist tradition has taken something insightful (a powerful appreciation of the personal role of the spiritual teacher) and betrayed those insights by imposing metaphysical assumptions on them. Again, the difficulties emerge when Buddhism does not actually base its knowledge on experience. When the guru becomes an absolute source of knowledge, whether due to his traditional role or due to his personal charisma, one's own experience is deliberately set aside, and abrogated if it conflicts with the guru's instructions. Forgetting that the guru's instructions are still interpreted through one's own experience, and that one needs to build up one's own sustainable picture rather than imposing an unsustainable higher command on oneself, the disciple fails to gain the objectivity that he/she could have gained with a more circumspect and less idealised approach to the guru.

If that is not enough, one should also consider the effects on the guru himself. Even a guru who starts off sincere and modest, when subjected to endless idealisation and veneration, never challenged and treated as an infallible fount of authority, is likely to end up with an inflated idea of himself. It is not good for anyone, and certainly not good for the objectivity of the guru (or of those he teaches) to be treated like that. Again, it would be odd for Buddhists to expect that positive conditioning works on people but negative does not, or that gurus are not as subject to conditioning as other people, however many spiritual strengths they may begin with.

The trouble with scriptures

The idea of a canonical scripture in Buddhism is dependent on the belief in the enlightenment of the Buddha. An ancient scripture is given canonical authority if it is *Buddha vacana*, the word of the Buddha. In Theravada Buddhism, this is usually interpreted to mean the actual words of the historical Buddha, and thus the canonical status of a scripture depends on a claim about its historical authenticity. In Mahayana

Buddhism, Buddha vacana is more likely to be interpreted in non-historical terms, as whatever is conducive to enlightenment.

There is a widespread recognition in Buddhism that scriptures are limited vehicles for conveying the truth. Enlightenment is often said to be beyond words, so that words can only offer pointers in the direction of enlightenment. Textual fundamentalism is not impossible[8], but it is unusual, particularly amongst Western Buddhists. Nevertheless, there is a canon of scriptures that is venerated and given special status because of the connection it is believed to have with enlightenment. The fact that their status is not absolute should not deter us from asking critical questions about the status of scriptures, and the authority given them as sources of knowledge.

If, as in the Theravada, scriptures are given canonical status because of the belief that they represent the words of the historical Buddha, it is clear that the belief in their special value as a source of knowledge depends on a revelatory appeal to the Buddha's enlightenment. Buddhists may protest that this "revelation" does not depend

---

[8] See *Buddhist Fundamentalism and MinorityIdentities in Sri Lanka* Tessa Bartholomeusz and Chandra Richard de Silva, State University of New York Press (1998)

on the same assumptions as a revelation from God, but nevertheless the fact that they mark certain scriptures out as the word of the Buddha shows that the idea of revelation must be working in some respect.

It is possible to believe in a revelation from the Buddha and yet recognise the scripture as an imperfect verbal formulation, which we will also understand imperfectly. Buddhists may, indeed, claim that their canonical scriptures only offer good advice, to which they pay special attention because of its believed origin from the Buddha. Yet how many pieces of mere good advice are carefully preserved over 2000 years or more, memorised, exhaustively studied and commented on, venerated and turned into objects of worship? If they were the only possible pieces of good advice, this might be plausible, but given the many other pieces of good advice there are available which are not given the same kind of treatment, it becomes obvious that the reason Buddhists treat their scriptures in this way is merely due to their adherence to a cultural tradition, and has little to do with any unique features of the texts themselves.

This becomes even clearer in the case of the Mahayana approach. At least some Mahayanists claim that the appeal to the historical Buddha can be dispensed with, even if they like to keep up some kind of symbolic connection with him. This means that the justification for the special status of the scriptures is, in theory, purely one of how useful they are in practice. If this were really the case, however, Mahayanists ought to be constantly on the lookout for new candidates for their canons, and any book with a high level of useful spiritual content, regardless of its origin, should be included. However, this is far from being the case. In practice, Mahayanists maintain a closed canon based on cultural tradition.

If Buddhists do not in fact treat their scriptures as revelations, the whole idea of a canon becomes redundant. If scriptures merely offered good and useful advice, not only would this cross cultural and religious barriers, but it would vary in intensity. Rather than justifying a single kind of judgement that a scripture is "canonical" (or Buddha vacana), the differing degrees of usefulness of the advice would justify different degrees of credit.

None of this is intended to suggest that the Buddhist scriptures do not, in fact, contain much useful advice. For example, there are instructions on meditation, ethical guidance, and glimpses of the Buddha as an inspiring character. The trouble with Buddhist scriptures consists only in the status given to them and its implications. Just as the Bible contains embarrassing bits (such as Lot offering his daughters' virginity to a lustful mob, or God commanding the genocide of the Amalekites) that Christians might often wish were not there so they would not have to explain them away, the Buddhist canons also contain sections which are frankly an embarrassment to anyone who wants to in any way claim them as part of an authoritative set of documents. In the Buddhist canonical literature, for example, there is the story of Prince Vessantara, who sells his wife and children into slavery through supposedly exemplary non-attachment[9], there is the story of another exemplary prince who feeds himself to a hungry tigress[10], and there is the extremely crude defence of rebirth by the setting up of the stubborn and stupid "sceptic" Prince Payasi as a straw man to argue against it with ludicrous ineffectiveness[11]. If these passages were not given a special authoritative status by the fact of their being regarded as canonical, none of this need be

---

[9] Cariyapitaka, translated by I.B. Horner, included in *Minor Anthologies of the Pali Canon,* Part III (Pali Text Society, 1975), I.9
[10] Vyaghri Jataka, *Jatakamala* no. 1
[11] Payasi Sutta, Digha Nikaya sutta 23

an issue, but the canonisation of mixed traditional material creates arguments over such passages.

Buddhism has betrayed its own insights by not being able to jettison such material, and by continuing to give it authoritative status. The fact that Buddhists interpret this authoritative scriptural status in different ways, and will in practice use some bits of the canon much more than others, does not change the central point here – that having a canon at all is a mark of dogmatic assumptions. Buddhists cannot and should not accept claims as true just because they are in the canon, and therefore the way the canon should be regarded is no different from any other document – it should be judged in relation to experience using the Middle Way. So the existence of the canon and the special status of scriptures is either indefensible or it is redundant. Although what scriptures contain may be a useful source of information or guidance, this has nothing to do with them being scriptures.

One standard Buddhist response to this is to say that the type of authority that Buddhists place in their scriptures differs from the nature of scriptural authority in other religions. They might say that the authority of scriptures merely justifies giving them high regard, or a kind of *prima facie* authority – to be turned to first given the trust that Buddhists have in the Buddha as a previously useful source of advice. It is similar, perhaps, to trusting a weather forecaster that one has known to be correct in the past. This past experience of positive benefit from the advice of the Buddha is said to justify turning to the Buddhist scriptures, which are records of the Buddha's words (or perhaps those of other enlightened followers of the Buddha), just as one would turn first to the reliable weather forecaster if one wanted a reliable weather forecast.

The trouble with the idea that *trusting* the scriptures is at all like trusting a reliable person is that it does not take into account the huge differences between the two situations. To judge a person reliable in one's own experience, one can not only consult the pattern of what one has directly and personally experienced, but also the personal intuitions and the contextual factors. A local farmer who is a good weather forecaster will not only be known personally, but also will be basing his forecasts on a knowledge of the same local environment that I live in. He will also be making claims on a relatively straightforward matter where the scope for misunderstanding is limited. If I am a friend of his, I am also likely to be more charitable in my interpretations of situations where he might be judged wrong.

However, in the case of the Buddha, we do not meet him personally or directly in scriptures, but only as mediated by a 2,500-year-old tradition. We meet the Buddha that that tradition wishes to present to us, by necessity a highly selective and possibly distorted picture. He is speaking in the language and cultural context of ancient India, a cultural context very different from our own. To believe in the veracity of claims made in these circumstances is not a question of trust, but of faith. It is not supported by personal experience, contextual immediacy or even an assurance of accuracy.

Another possible response to this problem is to see it purely as a question about the historical accuracy of Buddhist scriptures, and try to provide scholarly answers. Scholarship can provide a limited amount of information to help us understand the context of the scriptures, their original intention and purpose, and the ways in which problems of language or transmission might distort our understanding of them. However, many scholarly assertions are in any case composed of guesswork based on necessarily limited evidence. No amount of scholarship is likely to be able to remove the alien cultural origins and the remoteness of Buddhist scriptures. It is possible to understand some aspects of the context in which the Buddha spoke, but not apply it relevantly to our own time, nor know how to do so. Merely understanding the aspects of the context that we are able to trace at this distance is not enough to do much to bridge the gap, especially when these are not ordinary documents, but ones that are having special reliance placed on them.

Furthermore, a preoccupation with solving the problem of the source of knowledge in Buddhism through the scholarly investigation of scriptures often seems to have the effect of digging Buddhists deeper and deeper into certain framing assumptions. The detailed investigation of traditional sources only reinforces the idea that they are a true source of knowledge, leading either to the acceptance or rejection of Buddhism purely on traditional grounds. Scholars, who seem on the face of it to be engaging in an objective scientific investigation of the objectivity of Buddhism, are often amongst the strongest conservative influences, as they keep the focus on traditional "Buddhism" as a field of study, rather than considering its claims in a larger practical and philosophical context.

Scholarly investigation of scriptures and their background also very rapidly becomes an end in itself, and a massive distraction from the insights offered by the texts. To understand the ideas in what is taken to be their "genuine" original form, the scholarly study of scriptures (whether done by Buddhists or by non-Buddhist academics) requires careful study of the context. All the attention is then given to "what is really being said" (as though we really had any access to that!) rather than to the critical evaluation or adaptation of the insightful ideas to be found in Buddhist scriptures.

In a self-fulfilling circle, the Buddhist scholar also sets out to find truths in scriptures and finds them there, but these "truths" are framed and created by the fact that they are in the scriptures, rather than being judged by any external needs and compared with other possible sources of insight. On many occasions, a Buddhist undertaking the study of scriptures has already abandoned any recognition that he/she is constructing insights for him/herself, but is looking for ones already there in the words of the scripture in a fashion which, judged only on Buddhist principles, must be deluded.

For all these reasons, scriptures are not a reliable source of knowledge in Buddhism. Where they offer understanding or insight, the value of these insights has to be judged according to other standards that do not originate in the scripture or its status. The belief in a canonical standard in Buddhism depends on metaphysical assumptions about enlightenment as revelation, which are at odds with some of the key insights in Buddhism. Scholarly study, which some Buddhists and others undertake as a way of overcoming these difficulties, is not at all able to overcome them, and in many ways only operates as a distraction from the underlying philosophical issues that surround Buddhism and which remain unexamined. Finally, although a critique of scriptures and a recognition of their limitations exist in Buddhism, these are largely not consistently applied, otherwise there would not be the same faith in scriptures that exists in many Buddhists.

Chapter 3: The constraint of compassion

The next few chapters after this are going to be concerned with Buddhist doctrines, and the huge unnecessary problems caused by Buddhist metaphysics. In reading this it would be easy to get things out of perspective and lose the sense of a balanced critique of Buddhism. So, before plunging into criticism of karma, rebirth, dependent origination, and the like I would like to give some attention to an area where I think Buddhism is stronger and has much to offer the world – the area of love and compassion. This does not mean that the going is smooth, or that Buddhists seem to have entirely succeeded in their aims in this area. There are weaknesses to be considered here too, which I would see as constraints on Buddhist success in cultivating and applying love. However, it is much easier to be sympathetic to Buddhism when it promotes the cultivation of positive emotions than when it puts forward dogmas.

The cultivation of love

In the Buddhist tradition going back to the Buddha, there are four *brahma-viharas*, or positive emotions, which Buddhists are advised to cultivate as an important aspect of their spiritual path. These four positive emotions are love or loving-kindness (*metta*), compassion (*karuna*), sympathetic joy (*mudita*) and equanimity (*upeksa*)[12]. What underlies all of these is a positive emotional response of consistently willing good towards both oneself and others, whether they are suffering or rejoicing. This positive emotion needs to be consistent, impartial and unconditional, not due to an attachment to an idea of what one can get back from others, nor in response to their attractive qualities. Each of the positive emotions is cultivated systematically through a meditation practice, which gradually aims to broaden positive sympathies that already exist.

The great strength that Buddhism offers here is the possibility of *cultivating* love. In comparison with Christianity, for example, Buddhism seems to offer a much more practical approach to love, less dependent on metaphysical beliefs. Christianity celebrates love a great deal, but regards it as a gift of God rather than as a mental state possessed by human beings. Buddhism, on the other hand, shows an effort to get to

---

[12] For more information, see, for example, Sharon Salzberg, *Loving-kindness* (Shambhala 1995)

grips with the conditions that actually give rise to love in the human mind, and also those that take it away again.

Another strength that Buddhism offers here is a recognition of the importance of self-love. The *metta-bhavana* (cultivation of loving-kindness) meditation, like the similar meditations on the other three positive emotions, begins with the cultivation of love towards oneself. In this respect Buddhism is not unique, as Western psychology has independently reached a widespread understanding of the importance of self-esteem to the basic psychological health of the individual. However, it provides an additional voice against the deeply mistaken view still widespread in the world, that love consists in self-abnegation and the alienated renunciation of one's own interests. The central symbol of Christianity, the crucifixion, often seems to be understood as conveying the message that love is self-sacrificial. The positive value of Buddhism simply pointing out that love is not a brand of masochism cannot be underestimated.

Broadly speaking, love in Buddhism is seen as needing to be in balance with wisdom, an insight which accords fully with the Middle Way. Love without wisdom is mere sentimentality, which does not take into account the context or the consequences of love. On the other hand, wisdom without love is impotent. It is possible to have a good understanding of conditions, but for this understanding to be merely abstract and not to motivate action. Love is part of the emotional state of the organism, which can actually drive us to reach out rather than remain in our habitual behaviour.

Love, then, is a central aspect of the Middle Way, the emotional aspect of the way in which one gets to grips with conditions. One can get to grips with one's own bad habits only by caring about oneself. One becomes involved with the life of others, beyond simply making use of them, only when motivated by love for them. Even animals, plants, places or the world in general can be objects of love, motivating action to protect them.

However, unfortunately in this area as in others Buddhism can be its own worst enemy – indeed has not shown sufficient care for its own welfare to be consistent. There are some confusions in the ways in which Buddhists often understand love, which are often supported by the contradictory ways in which the Buddhist tradition presents it. These are not very surprising given the contradictions examined elsewhere in this book, which spill over into the treatment of love. I will be examining two aspects of this treatment. One is in the idealised way in which the importance of love can be presented, which is linked to a continuing vein of asceticism in the Buddhist treatment of love. The other area concerns the troubled and complex relationship between love, self-regard, and the individual.

The constraint of the ideal

Most of us, in our better moments, would like to love more than we do. Yet we are beset with conditionings that work against love. We are competitive creatures apparently programmed by evolution to take advantage of the weaknesses of others rather than to support them. Our love grows most easily from a conscious or unconscious calculation of advantage, not from a pure goodwill. It is much easier to love a pretty girl than a drunken football hooligan. Not just greed and hatred, but also physical conditions, hold us back from loving ourselves and loving others.

In balancing compassion with wisdom, also, we must limit the expression of our love to the small field that is feasible. Even if in some sense we are able to love all, we cannot aid all, and can often do very little for others without substantially encroaching on things that we value for ourselves, such as time or money. Our love would be fruitless if it was not focused on a few specific people, or specific actions, in our experience.

The love that springs from the Middle Way then, would be a realistic love which advances step-by-step to allow us to gradually loosen the narrowness of our sympathies. The *metta-bhavana* meditation works in exactly this way, beginning with reflection on those that we find it easier to love, such as a good friend, and working outwards to broaden that love to an enemy. Yet one of the major faults in Buddhism is that the ideals presented rarely accord with this model of love. The figures that represent love, and are the objects of worship or the models intended to inspire us to love, are not figures that inspire us to move forward from where we are, but are absolute idealisations of a love which has almost no relationship to our experience.

The Bodhisattva of compassion in Mahayana Buddhism, Avalokiteshvara, is frequently represented as having a thousand arms and ten heads, so as to be able to help more people through his limitless compassion. I only have 998 arms and nine heads to go to be like him! One of the Jataka stories describes the great compassion of the Buddha in one of his previous births, where he fed himself to a starving tigress[13]. The Bodhisattva Ideal in the Mahayana requires a vow, taken seriously by many practitioners, to save all sentient beings from all suffering.

Many Buddhists will protest here that these are symbols that represent compassion in its extreme or pure form: they are not intended to be "taken literally". However, the problem lies not in using symbolic or poetic forms of expression, but in misrepresentation of the object through that symbolic or poetic form of expression. It is not human love, and certainly not compassion balanced with wisdom, that is being symbolically or poetically represented, but a grotesque caricature of love. Such caricatures are presented so frequently in Buddhism that people are very likely to think that they represent what love really is, and that what they do is just a pale copy of it. This gets everything the wrong way round: what *they* do is real love, and it is the grotesque caricatures sanctioned by tradition that are not just pale copies but major distortions of it. In Buddhist scriptures, real convincing stories of people making little shifts forward

---

[13] Vyaghri Jataka, *Jatakamala* no. 1

from the narrowness of ego do exist (the story of Kisagotami in the Pali Canon is one example), but it is not these kinds of stories that get the major emphasis in representing the values of Buddhism, even though it is these that might actually inspire people towards a love which they could actually practice.

This absolutist distortion is closely associated with the continuing ascetic streak in Buddhism, which often makes nonsense of the idea that Buddhist practice begins with loving yourself. The Tibetan yogi Milarepa retires to a freezing cave and lives only on nettle soup[14]. Bodhidharma, the legendary founder of Zen in China, cuts off his eyelids to avoid falling asleep in meditation[15]. Chinese monks and nuns burn candles on the top of their heads to be initiated into bodhisattvahood[16]. Even today, the Tendai monks of Mount Hiei in Japan put themselves through months of gruelling

---

[14] See *Tibet's Great Yogi Milarepa*, ed. W.Y. Evans-Wentz, Oxford 1969

[15] See Maguire, Jack, *Essential Buddhism*, Pocket Books (2001)

[16] See Karma Lekshe Tsomo *Into the Jaws of Yama*, at http://www.scribd.com/doc/9978364/Karma-Lekshe-Tsomo-Into-the-Jaws-of-Yama-Lord-of-Death-Buddhism-Bioethics-And-Death : "Receiving three or more burns on the head is an integral part of the full ordination ceremony for Chinese monks and nuns."

marathon walks, followed by a fast that brings them close to death[17]. Buddhists generally do not go out of their way to distance themselves from such practices, but are apparently happy to see them represent Buddhist teachings despite their complete incompatibility with the Middle Way.

A natural response when confronted with constant idealisation is alienation. Because the ideals being constantly presented do not match one's own experience, and yet are also being presented as an important part of the values of the Buddhist group, one disassociates from them. Either one switches off and resigns oneself to not relating much to these ideals, although one accepts them "in principle", or one actually experiences emotional reactions against them. For many Buddhists, however, such reactions are simply part of practice, to be ridden through in the faith that one's mind will eventually become more tractable. When the culture of Buddhist practice is set up so that one is led to constantly blame oneself and one's unenlightened mind for all difficulties, it does not occur to anyone to realise that there may be something wrong with the ideals being presented. Thus

---

[17] See John Stevens, *The Marathon Monks of Mt. Hiei*, Shambhala 1988

dogmatic metaphysics exerts its stranglehold.

Of course there are some people who manage to work successfully with these absolute ideals and find them inspiring, but only because they manage to associate them with aspects of their own experience. For every Western Buddhist who manages this, there are several who are either put off at an early stage, or continue to accept alienated idealisations as the price of group membership.

At other times, real work is going on, and Buddhists are cultivating love through patient and systematic meditation, but thus is this real love constrained by ideals.

The division of love

The idealisation of love and the continuation of the ascetic tradition in Buddhism causes one kind of constraint to the development of love. Another, however, arises from a more fundamental conceptual problem, which I will call "the division of love". The division of love arises from the distinction I have already mentioned in chapter 1, between greed (or craving) on the one hand, and *dharma-*

chanda or desire for enlightenment on the other.

On the face of it, love is just greed. "I love her" can mean "I want to have sex with her", and "I love chocolate biscuits" means "I want to eat chocolate biscuits". Love in one common sense is just a desire to possess, to bolster one's ego by making the loved thing or person part of oneself. However, the Buddhist loving-kindness, or *metta* is conceived as *qualitatively* different from this. The kind of love Buddhism wants us to cultivate is universal, open, expects nothing back, and flows regardless of the attractive or unattractive aspects of the loved object. So, love in Buddhism is qualitatively divided into two types, good love and bad love.

The problem with this is that it does not fully accord with our experience. There may be a few examples of obviously crude greed and a few examples of obviously pure universal love, but the vast majority of the feelings we have are mixed. For example, my motives for writing this book are mixed: I would genuinely like to do good for other human beings by helping them to understand the pros and cons of Buddhism, so in some ways this book is an expression of *metta*. On the other hand, I would also like the book to be a success and for people to admire it and even pay me money for it (greed), and I would like the egoistic satisfaction of people whom I disagree with realising the error of their views (hatred, or inverted greed). Nearly everything we do is similarly mixed.

Of course, in practice Buddhists often recognise this, and apply the ideal of metta to their experience with care and discrimination. However, my impression is that the division in the concept of love that they are using frequently undermines this. One example of this would be the rejection of romantic love and the love of children, both of which have very mixed motives. Whilst the Buddha himself gave advice to lay people about duties in the lay life[18], at the same time this was in a context that clearly made this kind of love second-class compared to the monastic practice of leaving the family. Traditional Buddhism helps people to make the best of worldly love, but does not recognise worldly love as on a continuum with properly disinterested *metta*.

This is not just a point about the tradition of monasticism: rather monasticism itself depends on the division of love for its justification. The division of love continues even in those forms of Buddhism (such as

---

[18] For example, the Sigalavada Sutta (Digha Nikaya sutta 31)

the FWBO or Triratna Buddhist Community) that have abandoned monasticism, as evidenced, for example, by Sangharakshita's attacks on romantic love. As Sangharakshita writes, "The 'couple' is the enemy of the spiritual community. By the couple, in this context, one means two people, usually of the opposite sex, who are neurotically dependent on each other and whose relationship, therefore, is one of mutual exploitation and mutual addiction....Their 'presence' within the spiritual community can only have a disruptive effect."[19] In drawing attention to the neurotic elements in Romantic love, Sangharakshita typically overstates his case and perpetuates the idea that Romantic love is of a discontinuously different *type* to real spiritual love.

A different conceptual model is needed, not just a change in practices still appealing to the old model, because in that way the contradictions between practice and the old model will continue to assert themselves. The new model, I would suggest, should be to see the difference between metta and greed as a matter of degree rather than a single clear-cut distinction. Love can be more or less disinterested and more or less universal. In other words, love can be more

---

[19] Sangharakshita, Alternative Traditions, Windhorse Publications, p.180

or less wise and more or less attuned to conditions. The most narrow and possessive forms of romantic love, for example, are not different from metta in any essential way, but only in the extent of the conditions they take into account. They are less attuned to conditions because they prevent the psychological and spiritual needs of both partners from being addressed.

The language used makes a big difference here. If you talk about "metta" and "love" as two different things, people will tend to assume that they *are* two different things. If, on the other hand, you use a single word, "love", to cover the entire spectrum, people are much more likely to recognise the continuity between one kind of love and another.

A more useful model of love, I would suggest, would also see the distinctions between more helpful and less helpful forms of love as *quantitative* rather than *qualitative*. The same love is involved in each case, but the more helpful forms are more integrated. This means that the emotional energies which love consists in are working together more harmoniously towards longer-term goals. To take a simple example, the possessive love of a jealous husband is not *bad* or different in quality from universal goodwill, it is just badly directed because it is in conflict with the real goodwill he also feels towards his wife. He wants her to be happy, but at the same time he wants to restrict her life in a way which will interfere with her happiness. The two things that he wants are in conflict, and he could integrate his love better by applying wisdom to see that his love is better served in the longer term by letting go of his jealousy. If he succeeds in doing this, it is not that the nature of his love has changed, only that more of the energy of which it consists is now working together.

In the course of Buddhist meditation (particularly meditation that cultivates positive emotion), one is often advised to recognise and accept one's feelings. It is a basic psychological insight that one can only transform a feeling positively after having fully recognised it as it is. However, we cease to do this if we carry round a model that labels those feelings as in any way bad, second-class, or inferior. If the management of a factory were to instruct two different sets of workers to make different parts which are ultimately intended to fit together into a single device, and the workers followed their instructions, but due to bad design the two parts did not fit together to fulfil the intended purpose, then it is not the worker's fault, but the management's. We should not blame our feelings, which are like the workers, for doing their job. Feelings are just energy. However, we may well need to manage them better.

Self and ego

Before leaving the topic of love, I would also like to apply the point about the division of love to the question of self-love. One of the ways that the division of love can be unhelpfully applied is by seeing greed as "selfish" and metta as "unselfish". The unhelpful division of love in the Buddhist tradition also gets closely interlocked with traditional unhelpful ways of thinking about the self in Western thought. This area is fraught by confusion of terminology, with different commentators using the terms "self", "ego" and "individual" differently. I am just going to stipulate the way in which I would like to use these terms.

In the way I would prefer to use the terms, "individual" refers to a single person inhabiting a single human body. "Self" refers to that individual body and mind as we think of it, so "self-love" means love of that individual body and mind I think of as my own. "Selfishness" refers to a narrow identification with my individual body and mind to the exclusion of others, and "selflessness" the opposite.

Where confusion rapidly sets in is if individual and self are not distinguished from what I prefer to call "ego". Ego consists in a set of identifications or volitions, of greed and hatred. I might identify with my own success and my own possessions as an individual, but I might also identify with relatives, friends, country, religion, ideas etc. If I identify with my national football team, for example, and they lose, my ego is hurt, even though I as an individual have not been affected at all.

Where does love lie in this? If we follow the Middle Way, and try to think of love as something that exists in our experience, rather than as an abstract metaphysical quantity, love cannot be any kind of reversal or denial of the ego. For ego motivates all our feelings and actions to varying extents: we cannot simply turn off the ego. If we think we have done so we are likely to be deceiving ourselves, for our ego identifies with the new policy as well as the old, and has merely shifted its understanding of the interests of what it identifies with. Thus self-control, if I choose not to be angry or not to reach for another cream bun, is not a reversal of the ego, but just the ego thinking longer-term.

The Middle Way cannot justify thinking of love as a reversal of the ego, but on the other hand it also cannot justify the nihilistic approach of thinking that we are stuck with the ego as it is and can do nothing to improve our actions. Either of these two approaches would involve imposing a dogmatic metaphysical idea on our experience. So, love needs to be thought of not as a reversal of the ego, but *as a loosening and extending of the ego's identifications*. If, for example, in the *metta-bhavana* meditation to cultivate loving-kindness, I start with a good friend, and then try to recognise the humanity that this friend has in common with my greatest enemy, I may start to extend the identification that I have with my friend to also cover the enemy. By loving my enemy, I am not giving anything up or squashing any other feelings, but merely extending feelings that already existed and allowing them to grow.

But now let's turn back to the issues associated with self and other. The relationship between ego and self is entirely contingent. Many of us do identify strongly with ourselves as individuals, but this is not a foregone conclusion. Parents, for example, are likely to identify strongly with their children. Some people, particularly women, can fall into the habit of not identifying with themselves very much, but only with others. The cultivation of love involves loosening and extending whatever ego identifications we have to start with, and this might involve loving ourselves more than we did before, as well as extending our identification from people we already identify with (such as lovers or children) to others towards whom we were previously indifferent or hostile.

Love, therefore, has nothing to do with *selfishness* or *selflessness*. By using these terms we just create confusion and probably resentment. Is it "selfish" to go on solitary retreat? Yes, because one is concerned with oneself and is not relating to others. However, one may be using such a period of withdrawal from social contact to loosen and extend ego-identifications and develop love. Since "selfish" in normal English usage confuses the ideas of loving oneself and being narrowly egoistic, it is much better avoided altogether. The same goes for *selflessness* and *self-sacrifice*, which in practice can often be extremely egoistic. The suicide bomber is extremely selfless, but can hardly be described as loving.

All of this approach seems to me to be very much in the spirit of the *metta-bhavana* and of the ways that Buddhist practice works with the self and ego. Through centuries of practice, Buddhist tradition has developed spiritual and psychological technologies which can be extremely effective. As often, however, there is interference and confusion of this picture from a Buddhist tradition that is not entirely in harmony with it.

This confusion arises particularly from continuing ascetic influence, which I have already mentioned earlier in part b of this chapter. The mistake in asceticism, as discovered by the Buddha in reaching his Middle Way, lies in trying to overcome the self rather than the ego, and also often in seeing this as an opposition rather than a loosening and extension. All too easily the tradition of renunciation in Buddhism – for example renouncing the household life to become a monk, can become an attack on one's life as it has been constructed so far rather than an attempt to loosen the boundaries of its identification. Monastic celibacy provides one example, which I will discuss further in chapter 10. It is difficult to see "going forth from home into homelessness" (the traditional formula for becoming a monk) as an act of love, when it wrenches away not only others but one's own identification with them: though there may be occasions when some household lives are so negative or fail to engage with conditions so much that it becomes so.

It is striking, also, how much less successful the Buddhist tradition has been in outward expressions of charitable motivation than the Christian one, despite the deep confusion in the Christian tradition between love and selflessness. Of course, there are Buddhists doing extremely successful altruistic work, and "engaged Buddhism" is a growing movement. But why did Buddhism need to be "engaged", and why was it not engaged already? Why, for that matter, was it not Buddhist lands that first developed modern medicine, the welfare state, and universal education? The answers to such big questions can only be offered in broad-brush terms, but here is one possible broad answer. It is not because Buddhists are "selfish" or engage in more individual practice, for this generally helps them to engage more in the conditions of love, not less. Instead, it is because their practice has been much too caught up in idealisations of love and emotions directed towards those idealisations, and not sufficiently on applying that love in practice by engaging with conditions.

Here is an example of this. A traditional Tibetan practitioner visualises the figure of Tara every day. With much practice he positively glows with love for all that he meets. On the other hand, a Christian missionary doctor does a little desultory prayer every morning, but actually spends most of his time and energy on running a clinic which improves the health of thousands of Africans. It is the Buddhist here who is more loving, but the Christian whose love is more effective. The Buddhist has a better understanding of the Middle Way, yet the Christian practises it more by addressing conditions more fully.

These figures are of course just representatives. There are vigorous practical Buddhists doing medical or social work and there are idealising contemplative Christians. Yet broadly I would argue that these two figures are more representative of their respective traditions than otherwise. What has gone wrong for the Buddhist is not selfishness, but a situation in which feelings of love have become an end in themselves, rather than being part of a wider project to address conditions. This may, in the end, be because what the Buddhist seeks is not to address conditions, but to achieve enlightenment, a condition which is understood primarily as a transformation of mental states rather than outward conditions.

If love is the loosening and extending of ego-identifications and is to be seen quantitatively rather than qualitatively, those identifications are concerned just as much with the physical conditions of the world and with society as with the self. The Christian and the Buddhist in this example are both working with conditions, and extending egoistic identifications in the process, but the Buddhist has limited the range of conditions addressed, and thus limited the impact of Buddhism on the world.

In conclusion to this chapter on love, then, I have argued that Buddhism has some important insights into the practical cultivation of love, and that this continues to occur amongst Buddhists. However, this cultivation of love is unnecessarily constrained by several interrelated factors: the idealisation of love in forms remote from common experience, the continuing influence of asceticism in despite of the Middle Way, the division in Buddhist thinking between universal and worldly love, and the tendency (created by the other factors) to think of love as in opposition to the self. It is the reform of these ways of thinking about love that could help remove some of the constraints on compassion in Buddhism, perhaps including those which limit its contribution to the relief of suffering in the world when compared to other major religions.

Chapter 4: The trouble with karma

Cosmic house points

Karma (or *kamma* in Pali) is often understood to be an essential belief of Buddhism. Traditionally, it is understood as the basis of Buddhist morality. Karma provides the mechanism whereby greed, hatred and ignorance give rise to unsatisfactoriness through the conditioning effects of habitual mental states. According to the law of karma, an action (including a mental action) performed under the influence of greed, hatred and ignorance will always give rise to undesirable consequences for the person performing the action. The consequences of "good" actions will be "good" in worldly terms, leading to a more pleasant and advantageous position in the world, whilst "bad" karma leads to a worse position. All karma, however, is ultimately bad in the sense that it leads to the continuance of unenlightened existence. An enlightened person is no longer producing any new karma, and only continues on earth as a result of previous karma which is still working itself out[20].

There are a variety of interpretations of karma and its effects in the Buddhist world. The most common, and traditional, view in both Theravada and Tibetan Buddhism is that all our experience is the result of our karma. Whatever conditions affect us now, be they rainstorms, lottery wins or a sudden hostility from a colleague, are on this account due to our previous actions. We live in a world entirely of our own making, no more and no less than we deserve. I will refer to this as the "traditional view of karma".

The alternative view of karma put forward by some Western Buddhists, such as Sangharakshita[21], still sees all our actions as giving rise to equivalent effects. However, this reformed view does not accept that all our experiences are due to past karma.

---

[20] For a sensible Western Buddhist attempt to clarify these teachings see *Exploring Karma and Rebirth* by Nagapriya (Windhorse Publications 2004). Nagapriya considers some of the questions I raise in this chapter, but does not, to my mind, pursue them with enough rigour.

[21] Sangharakshita's view appeals to Buddhaghosha's commentary on the Abhidhamma and is discussed in Sangharakshita *The Three Jewels* p 69, *Transforming Self and World* p.204, and *Who is the Buddha?* P.105-7 (all published by Windhorse Publications)

Instead, this view takes there to be a range of possible types of conditioning at work, which include the types of conditioning recognised by science (such as physical, biological or psychological conditioning) as well as karmic conditioning. So, on this view we do not always get what we deserve. For example, we may be struck down by an infectious disease just because there is one going round, not because we deserve it as an effect of our previous actions. Nevertheless, if I have performed any action motivated by greed or hatred in the past, it will always have an effect on me in the future.

Buddhists in the West often like to distance this belief from the idea of "reward" and "punishment" from God as believed in by Christians and Muslims. For Buddhists the operation of karma is impersonal, being a kind of natural moral law, rather than the rewarding or punishing actions of a person. Nevertheless, the effect on the individual can be understood very much in terms of reward or punishment (which do not always require a personal intervention to be seen that way). Whatever you do that's good will have a good result, whilst whatever you do that's bad will have a bad result. This, it is believed, gives us a reason for being responsible for our actions. If we do not take responsibility for ourselves then we will suffer for it.

Whether you adopt the traditional or the reformed interpretation of the workings of karma, the central issues remain the same. The difficulties we might have in believing that we deserve everything that happens to us are only one of many problems with karma. The reformed view has dealt with that particular problem, allowing for the possibility of tragedy, and releasing Buddhists from the apparent need to defend undeserved suffering as somehow just. The more sensible Buddhists who take the reformed view at least do not have to argue that children who die of leukaemia must have done something wrong in a previous life. In this sense the reformed view is an advance on the traditional view, but it nevertheless leaves many problems with karma unresolved.

There is an apparently necessary link between belief in karma and belief in rebirth, because if one does not experience the good or bad effects of an action during this lifetime, then it is believed that the "left over" karma will instead either affect the nature of our next rebirth, or lead to other events affecting us in future lives. Given that we do not always seem to experience the bad effects of our actions during life (for example, brutal dictators live in happy retirement, and angelic people die unexpectedly from diseases or accidents), rebirth provides Buddhists with a let-out clause so that they can continue to believe in the law of karma no matter what we may experience.

This let-out clause alone makes it clear that belief in karma is a metaphysical belief not in accordance with the Middle Way. This alone might be enough to justify Buddhists in jettisoning all belief in both karma and rebirth. However, in my experience it rarely is. More conservative Buddhists simply accept karma and rebirth in the faith that the Buddha came to know the truth about them, and what he is supposed to have said must be ultimately right, to be finally understood when one gains enlightenment. More radical Buddhists sometimes say that they are agnostic about rebirth, and then defend karma by misleadingly reducing it to the practical realisation that "actions have consequences". We all certainly need to recognise that actions have consequences, and this point is central to basic moral reasoning. However, the law of karma claims much more than that actions have consequences: it claims that they unfailingly have equivalent consequences according to the nature of the action, even if those consequences may take many lifetimes to come to fruition. To take this traditional metaphysical doctrine and dress it up as a practical moral insight (apparently assuming that people can only really understand the nature of moral consequences if they accept the doctrine of karma) is one of the most dishonest things I have observed Western Buddhists doing – yet they do it routinely and it has become part of Western Buddhist culture. This obfuscation is one of the key ways that dogma finds its way into Western Buddhism by the back door.

However, the metaphysical nature of karma is only the central point, from which spring many other problems. One of the biggest of these is the type of mentality required to appeal to karma as the basis of moral responsibility. Under this mentality, we are motivated to act well out of concern for the rewards or punishments that will follow. In many British schools there is a system of "house points" that resembles this. If pupils behave well, and achieve the sorts of things teachers want them to achieve, then they get rewarded with house points, whereas if they are naughty they get them deducted. Awards and perhaps prizes may follow, in addition to praise, for gaining house points. This closed system of justice is very reassuring for children, though there are also some whom it inevitably fails to motivate. Arguably, this may be a good way to motivate many schoolchildren up to a certain age. However, as they advance into greater maturity the house points cease to have much effect, perhaps because many adolescents are developing their own, more mature, ways of judging the worth of their actions, or perhaps because they become much more interested in the judgements of their peers and less in those of teachers.

A system of rewards or punishments on a cosmic scale infantilises us all, and it is hardly surprising if it fails to motivate educated people in today's Western world. For one thing, it works on the assumption that "being good" can be reduced to a set of simple, clear rules in the way it can in a school. But adults live in a complex world full of contradictions between different "good" things. For example, going on retreat might be good for one's own state, but not good for one's family who don't want to be left behind. It is not even clear which of these conflicting actions would result in good karma. A right judgement here, based on the Middle Way, involves recognising and addressing that complexity in conditions. However, if you are trying to gain good karma you will be bound to oversimplify your picture of the situation in an anxiety to avoid breaking the rules. Belief in karma encourages a nursery-school picture of morality. It is hardly surprising if it has normally been accompanied in traditional Buddhism by an over-simplified ethics: a point I will return to in chapter 10.

For another thing, the law of karma leads us to assume that we will be motivated by the same sorts of consequences in future as the ones that affect us now. House points may have been a big deal at school, but they mean almost nothing after you have left. Similarly, the kinds of good or bad consequences for moral or immoral action that might make an impression on us currently may well seem irrelevant in future. Let's take an example episode under the law of karma. Let's say that one day, when filling in my tax return, I find a way of fiddling it undetected, and thus save myself a substantial amount of money through dishonest means, but am free from punishment by the law. Later in life, however, I become extremely non-attached to money, and no longer care very much about gaining it or losing it. At this point, however, the karmic consequence of my earlier dishonesty revisits me, in the form of someone else swindling me of the same amount of money I earlier swindled from the government in lost tax revenue. However, this loss really makes no impression on me, and can hardly be said to be a punishment equivalent to the loss I earlier inflicted on others.

It's possible to argue here about the idea of moral *equivalence* in the law of karma. Perhaps being swindled of the same amount of money is not really equivalent. However, the deeper problem here is that there *is* no acceptable basis for equivalence: I cannot be justly punished (or rewarded) for an action I did at a different time when I was different, because I am no longer the person who committed the offence. Human law naturally has to skate over this problem (although question are still raised about whether it is worth pursuing old war criminals for crimes they did fifty years ago), but karmic law, by its very nature, must be unfailingly just. It is this idea of justice that is imported from an over-simplified, infantilised universe and projected onto the one we actually inhabit. Absolute cosmic justice is not only against the evidence, it is actually contradictory in its very conception.

Again, I must repeat that it makes no difference to these contradictions whether the justice is administered by a person such as God, or just happens impersonally: karma would not serve its supposed function of supporting moral responsibility if it was not absolutely just. It also makes no difference how far you see karma as working through material processes in the universe or through the mind of a person. Even if karma is understood as operating entirely through the way we are in the habit of seeing things (e.g. if we see others as hateful, we interpret their behaviour as hating us) then the same problems stand. We do not know whether our future mental states are magically organised so as to reflect the effort we have put into the past ones. Experience suggests this is probably not the case, but that mental states are formed by many conditions rather than just past moral efforts, but in any case it would be impossible for the pleasure and pain we find in our future mental states to be precisely *just* in terms of our past mental efforts.

The "reformed" view of karma just makes the question of justice impossible to test in any way. It is claimed that our past mental efforts have an equivalent effect in the future, but we cannot tell when we have future experiences whether those have been formed by past karma or not. Thus the doctrine cannot even be put to the supposed "test" of an indefinite amount of future experience in the way that the traditional interpretation can. Although it manages to fudge the issue of just reward and punishment, the reformed view does so at the expense of becoming even more speculative and metaphysical, being purely a matter of faith in any event.

Of all the doctrines of Buddhism, karma has perhaps the least to be said for it and the most confusions attached to it. However, as with all the other doctrines there do seem to be some genuine insights behind it, and these genuine insights have continued to provide some of the basis of credibility according to which thoughtful Buddhists have accepted karma. The biggest of these is the recognition of the ways that our mental state, and our care for it or lack of care for it, can affect our future outlook and experience. If I give way to anger now, for example, I may make an enemy who will inflict pain on me in the future. Reflection on common experience is enough to make it clear that actions do generally lead to consequences, and that thoughtless actions quite often lead to negative consequences. The role of our mental states in these consequences quite often goes insufficiently recognised, and Buddhism quite rightly draws attention to these.

However, on the basis of these universal common insights Buddhism has erected an elaborate metaphysical edifice, and

Buddhism continues to present itself in a way that is misleading and contradictory because of this. Its long-term relationship with the more practical elements of Buddhism can perhaps only be explained by the importance of karma as a moral motivator in ancient Indian thought. Whether the Buddha was at fault in making use of this cultural structure in his own context is a complex question that I will not attempt to resolve here, but it is much clearer that the doctrine of karma has no relevance to our own time, and will certainly not inspire moral responsibility in our own time.

If one turns, instead, to the Middle Way as a source of moral responsibility, a much more universal conception can be found which is equally applicable to the Buddha's time and ours. Quite simply, moral responsibility consists in addressing conditions, rather than sheltering under metaphysical conceptions which prevent us from addressing conditions. To the extent that we do not address conditions, the potential of our lives will tend to remain unfulfilled. The virtue of living our lives in greater awareness of the conditions that surround us is its own reward.

One of the strongest artistic demonstrations of this I have come across is in the film

Groundhog Day. Here a man finds himself living the same day over and over again, and rapidly realises that this means there are no long-term consequences to his actions. It's true that his first response to this is the infantile one: he does forbidden things. However, after a while he realises that the only way to be happy in this situation is to interpret it positively. He then uses each day to practise so as to do the next one better, improving both his own skills and his care for others. He realises the benefits of goodness, not because of any beliefs about the good or bad consequences of his actions in this life or a future one, but because he is forced to focus more intensively on the period of time he is living in now.

Karma vs nirvana

Unfortunately, however, we are not yet finished with karma. What we have been discussing so far is established Buddhist doctrine, but it is only the established doctrine of one aspect of Buddhism: what is sometimes known as "karmic" or "popular" Buddhism. Side-by-side with the cosmic house points system is another sort of Buddhism with different, perhaps contradictory, goals and values: what may be called "nirvanic" or "monastic" Buddhism.

Many Buddhists may still feel that the previous section completely misses the point, because the ultimate goal of Buddhism is not to get "good" karma, but to get no karma at all. The state of nirvana modelled by the Buddha is already one of freedom from any attachment to the consequences of one's actions. As frequently, many of the criticisms given in the last section have been preceded by a spoiler in Buddhist doctrine itself.

The distinction between karmic and nirvanic Buddhism (terms first used by the sociologist Melford Spiro) can be strongly associated with the social division in traditional Buddhism between monks (or nuns) and laity. Monks seek nirvana, therefore their ethical practice is understood as involving different requirements from that of lay people, who only seek a better rebirth. For this reason, the rules followed by monks and nuns (the Vinaya) differ from the precepts followed by lay people: for example, monks and nuns should be completely celibate, whereas lay people are expected to marry and should only avoid sexual misconduct such as infidelity. Although the separation between monk and lay has sometimes been softened in the Mahayana, the underlying division of goals between good karma for most lay people and no karma for monks (sometimes extended to serious lay practitioners) still prevails in most schools.

However, there are some schools and movements (such as the FWBO/ Triratna Buddhist Community) that have abandoned the monk-lay division, particularly in the West. Although here the social situation that supported it has vanished, however, the gaping contradiction in Buddhist doctrine remains. How can one seek good karma and no karma at the same time? If one obeys the rules and is good, one is apparently digging oneself deeper into delusion, and only showing one's attachment to karmic rewards. If, on the other hand, one disregards the rules and tries to completely transcend all worldly concerns, one becomes apparently above and beyond all morality, and one's spiritual elevation seems to become completely disconnected from common human experience. For example, how can celibate monks preach to laypeople in favour of a sexual fidelity they may never have experienced, and which is, in terms of their own rules, an evil to be avoided?

One tempting solution to try to reconcile the two models is to see "good" karma as tapering-off, self-destructive karma. If one applies an incremental model, good karma is only relatively good because it helps you reach no karma at all. However, the best way to no karma at all would not be to do good deeds, but to do no deeds at all. Even when one takes into account the mental conditions for good karma, no mental deeds at all (just staying still and doing nothing, with no volitions and complete passivity) should be the quickest route to no karma. Of course, by the worldly standards of "good karma" this would not be desirable at all, but would be ducking one's responsibilities. There is no standard according to which good actions are a staging-post to no actions, apart from a contradictory standard.

The contradictory standard has been glued together so long by appeal to the authority of the Buddha. The Buddha clearly gave one sort of teachings to lay people and another to monks, but also softened the boundaries by encouraging monks to be compassionate and lay people to make limited renunciations. Buddhists through the ages have accepted the mystery of the contradiction, evidently in the hope that it would be resolved when they reached nirvana themselves. However, the effect of this has been simply to increase Buddhist dependency on the authority of the Buddha, and on faith rather than consistent reasoning. The mystery here is not of the sort that we need to accept because it would be unhelpful to try to find an answer (as in the case of the beginning of the universe), but simply a contradiction. Instead of helping us to address conditions through the recognition of our ignorance, this contradiction simply makes us more ignorant because it drives us into metaphysical beliefs about nirvana and the Buddha's revelation.

The alternative to accepting this contradiction is to decisively reject both the doctrine of karma and the doctrine of nirvana as they have been handed down. If we think of each of these only in terms that can be clearly understood within our own experience, they become practicable rather than confusing. If instead of a doctrine of karma we try to recognise ways that our mental states often have effects on our experience, and if instead of a doctrine of nirvana we simply recognise that progress is possible, nothing has been lost from Buddhist practice, except confusing conceptions which were weighing it down and unnecessarily putting people off.

Ridiculous rebirth

I ask myself if this heading is a little too strong. Is the appeal all in the alliteration? Rebirth may be mistaken, but is it really ridiculous? Unfortunately, I can only conclude that the answer is yes. Consider: here is a doctrine which is frequently presented in conflicting ways by the religion that produced it, but which even in its best-explained forms is incapable of playing the moral role it is traditionally believed to play. Nevertheless, Buddhists often continue to consider it central, and continue to seek evidence to support it, despite the fact that a little clear thinking would show that no evidence for it is possible. Perhaps even then, one might understand Buddhists adhering to such a teaching if it was of the slightest use, even if it was a convenient fiction. But no such usefulness can be attributed to believing in the doctrine of rebirth. Unlike any of the other doctrines I shall discuss in this book, there is really nothing positive at all to be said for it. Thus to call rebirth "ridiculous" is not an overstatement: it is better to laugh at it, simply because most Western Buddhists (even those who say they are "agnostic" about it, but would still prefer to believe in it if they could) take it far too seriously.

Let me begin with the first of these assertions. Buddhism presents rebirth in conflicting ways because it apparently cannot make up its mind whether or not rebirth consists of a person being reborn. One of the first things Buddhists are likely to say when the subject comes up is that rebirth should be distinguished from reincarnation, in which a soul passes from one body to another. In Buddhism, according to the official teaching, rebirth consists of a process of karmic conditioning, with each life causing the next in a similar fashion to a flame passing along a fuse. If we take this seriously then the doctrine of rebirth does not state that "I" am reborn, only that my actions set up patterns which may influence other people, who may in some respects resemble me, in the future.

At the same time, however, Buddhist scriptures are riddled with references to individual past rebirths, especially those of the Buddha, which he is said to have remembered at the time of his enlightenment. The Jataka stories, which are canonical Buddhist scriptures, give stories (many of them adapted folk tales) purporting to be those of the Buddha's previous lives, and precisely identifying not only who the Buddha was, but also often some of his leading disciples. Not only is this precise individuation of rebirth found in scripture and popular belief, but also in the official doctrines of Tibetan Buddhism, where tulkus or reincarnate lamas (such as the Dalai Lama) are said to continue, as the same individuals, in different bodies.

The only way out of this is to say that individuals should not really be identified in rebirth. Let us grant that the significant section of the Buddhist tradition which does this should not have done so, and that the official doctrine of the flame travelling along a fuse is what Buddhists should really believe. This doctrine may make rebirth compatible with anatta, but it still leaves us with a huge problem in attributing any moral continuity to a causal process. Why should a person in a new body who has inherited some habits from an old one "deserve" the effects of the habits of the previous person?

The Questions of King Milinda (a non-canonical early Buddhist text which attempts to tackle some tricky questions in Buddhist doctrine) explains this desert by making an analogy with a mango tree. It explains that a person who planted a mango deserves to eat the fruit off the ensuing mango tree, and a mango-thief would deserve punishment, even though the mango tree is not the same as the mango that was planted[22]. In the same way, it is claimed, a person who planted a karmic seed deserves to eat the fruit from it. The text appears to assume that the question is conclusively settled by this analogy, but there are many unjustifiable assumptions in it: it is not necessarily clear at all that I "deserve" the consequences of an action done long ago, especially when many other conditions contributed to it, and I myself may have changed a good deal in the meantime. I may have planted the mango on someone else's land, for example, and let them feed and water it. If I am reborn in the meantime, "I" will probably not even be able to remember planting the mango. Would I still deserve to eat the ensuing mangoes in such circumstances?

Once again, the model seems to be a closely controlled earthly justice system, but one applied in bizarre ways. Supposing I was a schoolchild who entered a new classroom and took over a desk belonging to another pupil the previous year: by inheriting the desk, however, for some reason I also inherit this person's house points. When I exclaim that this is irrational, it is explained to me that

---

[22] See *Questions of King Milinda* III,5,7; also anthologised in *Buddhist Scriptures* ed. Edward Conze, p.151 (Penguin 1959 – not to be confused with the totally different 2004 edition edited by Donald Lopez)

by sitting at the desk I will also be obliged to adopt some of this person's character: I will be near the front, so am likely to be more interested in gaining the teacher's attention, and the desk is covered in graffiti, so I am unlikely to take much pride in it. The fact that many other aspects of my character will not have been moulded by the desk appears to have eluded notice, just as the many other influences on a birth than karmic formations apparently count for nothing when it is considered what this new person deserves.

In short, rebirth cannot play the moral role it is believed to play by extending the payback time for karmic effects. If there are problems with the justice of any karmic payback system (as noted in the first section of this chapter), these problems redouble when the person being paid back is not in the same body, is not in any sense the same person, does not in most cases even remember the occasions for which he/she is supposedly being rewarded or punished, and has merely inherited some indeterminate karmic habits or patterns from a previous person. If Buddhists really believe all this, they should certainly no longer scoff at the promise of God in the book of Exodus, to punish those who break his commandments "up to the third or fourth generation". There is much more justification for paying the moral debts of one's great-grandfather than there is for being rewarded or punished on behalf of someone whose indeterminate habits have caused some of ours.

Despite all this, many Buddhists apparently continue to desire a belief in rebirth, and apparently wish they could have one if they haven't got one. To try to bolster this belief they look for evidence of rebirth. Various pieces of evidence have been offered, such as child memories of previous lives, adult memories gained under hypnosis, the remarkable abilities of child prodigies, or the predictions and tests of authenticity used for the identification of reborn tulkus (reincarnate lamas) in the Tibetan tradition.

I am not going to enter into any discussion of the strength of any of this supposed evidence, as it can be confidently stated on the basis of reasoning alone that it is a complete waste of time – at least as far as evidence for rebirth is concerned. These pieces of evidence may well provide intriguing indications of other unexplained phenomena, but their relationship to rebirth is completely contingent. Alternative explanations may be offered (including, but not limited to, reductive scientific explanations) for all these phenomena. One of the least frequently considered alternative explanations is that there are alternative ways in which elements of consciousness or habits may be floating around the universe in a random fashion. Even if it is correct that memories, consciousness, or karmic formations can in some fashion exist independently of the brain (a problematic enough assumption) there is no reason whatsoever to assume that they do so in accordance with a just karmic order in the universe, or that the karmic formations of one individual neatly cause those of another individual.

Just to give a few possibilities that are neither more nor less likely than rebirth as traditionally described: creatures on another planet may be sending thought waves which influence particular children, giving them unusual memories and abilities. Hypnosis may, by some unexplained mechanism, trigger someone else's past memories without the person under hypnosis being them in any respect. There may be a particular psychic power gained by certain Tibetan lamas which enables them to transfer their memories accurately to a child about to be born, again, without requiring them to in any sense *be* the child.

We are in pretty wacky territory here, but this is only to show that rebirth is one wacky theory out of many possible wacky theories, all of which explain the "evidence" available. The only reason to prefer rebirth to the other possible wacky theories is the sanction of tradition. The "evidence" in no way stands by itself, but is seized upon to help prop up faith in a pre-formed metaphysical system which has already been accepted as the desirable model before the discussion begins.

This takes us to the final point about whether belief in rebirth is desirable. In the end, those Western Buddhists who believe in it appear to do so because they want to believe in it, because they believe it will help them on their spiritual path if they believe in it. They are in a different situation to those traditional ethnic Buddhists who believe in rebirth unreflectively just because it is part of their cultural background. The Western Buddhist position is more similar to those post-Christians who really want to believe in God, even though they can't quite manage it. The idea that it is clearly helpful or desirable to believe in rebirth, however, is greatly mistaken.

The assumption that it is beneficial to believe in rebirth depends on the belief in karma, and the idea that believing in a complete law of karma, where all actions are paid back with equivalent consequences, motivates one in taking those consequences seriously. To be sufficiently concerned about my mental states and the actions they lead me into, it is thought, I need to be concerned about the effects that those states and actions will have on *me* in the future. To believe this fully I must also believe that even actions that are not paid back in this life will still affect me in a future life.

As a motivation, this is an extremely narrow one, of a kind that other Buddhist doctrines contradict. If I develop the Buddhist virtue of compassion, for example, I am likely to be concerned for others besides myself, not just my own future fate. If I take anatta seriously I should also not think of myself as continuing in a fixed form or gaining the rewards of karma. So, at one and the same time Buddhism apparently urges me to be concerned for *my* future fate, and also not to be concerned for my fate but to broaden my concerns. This is another example of the karma motivation conflicting with the nirvana motivation.

As a belief, the belief in rebirth also takes a lot of effort to hold and defend in a Western context. Most other people in Western society do not hold it, so I am likely to have to spend a lot of time defending it. Not only is this likely to create defensiveness and conflict, but the more strongly I hold it purely on the basis of faith, the more defensive I am likely to become. As with other metaphysical doctrines, the effects of holding this belief can often be negative, because they require a constriction of the ego to be held onto against the weight of argument and evidence.

So, far from being spiritually helpful, belief in rebirth seems much more likely to have the unhelpful effect of narrowing one's sympathies and rigidifying one's beliefs. In the face of all the contradictions and all the grounds for doubt, what is the point in hanging on to such a belief? It certainly has nothing to do with the central insights of Buddhism expressed in the Middle Way. The Middle Way requires the decisive rejection of metaphysics of the kind which the belief in rebirth exemplifies *par excellence*.

Buddhism without karma

After all this criticism, it might be a good idea to return to a positive note before concluding this chapter. What would Buddhism look like without the doctrine of karma? For many this idea is almost unimaginable, yet the idea of Buddhism without karma is far more coherent than the more commonly entertained idea of a Western Buddhism without rebirth but with karma.

The basic answer is simple: Buddhism without a doctrine of karma would be free to concentrate on asserting only the existence of probable moral consequences which we can actually experience, within a certain credible time frame. It is not difficult to trace the effects of hatred in producing more hatred, or of love in producing more love, within our experience. All we have to do is focus our attention on these processes, which is what practices of meditation and reflection in Buddhist tradition often do.

To believe in the *probability* that if I allow hatred for a certain person to develop, it will only lead to more hatred, is quite enough of a motivator for efforts to reduce hatred. Nor does the hatred necessarily have to have bad effects on me personally in the future, for imagining its bad effects on others might also motivate me.

A small shift, it might be thought, from talking about a universal law to talking about a probability traceable in experience. But the consequences of such a shift in Buddhist language should not be underestimated. Then, at last, it might be possible for Buddhists to get on with their useful practice without being distracted by argument about metaphysical claims, or being held back by attachments to ideas that have been dug in against experience.

In such an ideal future practice of Buddhism, the word "karma" would not appear, even in ritual. The word would not be fudged and modified and subjected to any other dishonest manipulation, but rather abandoned. Instead all Buddhists could pledge themselves wholeheartedly to the avoidance of the bad consequences which they are likely to experience from bad mental states and bad actions, whilst good consequences following from good mental states and good actions would be cultivated. How many more people might apply themselves to Buddhist practices if it could only become that straightforward! How much the world might benefit!

Chapter 5: The trouble with conditionality

What I actually mean here is "the trouble with the Buddhist doctrine of dependent origination or *pratityasamutpada*". However, that would not exactly make a very catchy chapter heading. There is nothing wrong with conditionality in itself, but it's the Buddhist view of it that needs unravelling.

The twelve links

The doctrine of dependent origination (or conditioned co-production) is often believed to be the most basic doctrine of Buddhism, putting forward a truth realised by the Buddha from which all other Buddhist teachings derive. There are two ways in which this doctrine is presented: as the twelve links (*nidanas*) which are illustrated by the outer ring of the Wheel of Samsara or "Wheel of Life", or as an underlying metaphysical principle. In both cases, the doctrine is intended to explain the workings of karma and of the second noble truth, to show how unenlightened existence is maintained and thus how it might be changed into enlightened existence. I will look at both of these ways of presenting dependent origination, starting with the twelve links.

The twelve links are intended to illustrate the conditioning process whereby delusion gives rise to unenlightened experience, unenlightened experience gives rise to greed, and greed gives rise to karmic effects, which in turn create the conditions for ignorance. Each of the twelve links represents a stage of conditioning, which then influences the next, and each is represented traditionally by a picture on the Wheel of Samsara. I am not going to go through a detailed explanation of all of the links here. Instead, any readers unfamiliar with them should refer to any of a number of introductions to Buddhism that explain them[23].

In brief, the twelve links can be divided into three phases, sometimes known as "past life", "present life" and "future life". The past life phase shows the process by which delusion produces karmic formations, karmic formations produce consciousness, the mind and body, and the five senses. In other words, it is only due to our lack of true

---

[23] For example, *The Buddhist Vision* by Alex Kennedy, (Rider 1985), which is structured around the Wheel of Samsara as a way of explaining Buddhist doctrines

understanding of reality that we act in such a way as to produce karma, and it is only due to karma that we have a body with the capacity for experience. The present life phase includes four stages: contact, feeling, craving and grasping. It illustrates how due to having bodies we come into contact with things around us and find them pleasant or unpleasant. If we react to pleasant things by wanting them and unpleasant things by rejecting them (craving) then we are led to grasp them, thus fixing them in a particular form in relation to ourselves. In the future life (which consists of becoming, birth and death) the results of this are seen. By grasping the world, we lead ourselves to be reborn in it after death, and by joining another life condemn ourselves to another round of birth and death and the perpetuation of delusion.

These twelve links map out the classic Buddhist vision of human conditioning. The exact form that they take is a matter of convention and is in some ways confusing: for each phase actually goes around the cycle in itself, so we have mentally gone through three revolutions of the cycle of unenlightened existence by the time we get to the end. Each phase includes prior conditions giving rise to karma, which then gives rise to more undesirable conditions.

Alternatively they may be seen as re-explaining the same process from three different points of view. Whatever the drawbacks of explaining the conditioning process in exactly this form, this is the one sanctioned by tradition because it is believed to have come from the Buddha. It thus seems unthinkable for most Buddhists to reform the twelve links so as to make them a bit clearer to the uninitiated: another example of the effects of belief in revelation from the Buddha.

One way of seeing the twelve links is as a teaching aid to explain karma and rebirth, which we have already discussed in the previous chapter. However, it also puts both karma and rebirth into the bigger context of a Buddhist metaphysical theory of the phenomenal universe, known as *pratityasamutpada* or dependent origination. Pratityasamutpada is the doctrine that all the unenlightened universe is conditioned (which I will discuss more later in this chapter), and the twelve links then go on to describe the exact form of conditioning we are subject to.

The "present life" phase of the twelve links also gives a more specific explanation of what might be seen as the biting point of the conditioning process. It is at the point of the link between feeling and craving that the next round of the conditioning process can arise again, unless we can alternatively avoid this next round through a spiritual effort. Craving (or greed) consists in the desire for more of something pleasant, or the desire to avoid something painful, and it is the experience of things as pleasant or painful which is referred to here as *feeling*. If we can simply experience a pleasant feeling as pleasant or a painful feeling as painful, and do so with awareness rather than with craving or aversion, it is claimed that we are able to shake ourselves free of this process. If we avoid the response of craving, we also avoid the ensuing link of grasping, where we try to possess something or push it away, and subsequently, if we go through this process sufficiently in our whole lives, we might also be able to avoid the next link, re-becoming, and hence the cycle of birth and death.

As in much of Buddhism, there seem to be genuine insights here that have then been over-extended and over-hyped. To experience pleasant, painful or neutral sensations and then just observe them without hanging onto them is an extremely useful technique constantly used in Buddhist meditation practice. It certainly does seem likely that, through effort, we can stop a process of addiction or obsession through this method. Craving (whether for food, another cigarette, to hit back at an offending person, or whatever) is a nervous response from an over-stimulated organism, and if we can relax our minds and bodies sufficiently and objectify our observation sufficiently, it often seems possible to stop that process. In this sense, the present phase of the twelve links identifies a psychological process that it is very valuable for all of us to know and work with.

The difficulties with this doctrine arise with its over-extension and the universal claims made for it. The traditional Buddhist account is that liberation is only possible between feeling and craving. Buddhist practice, then, consists of continually feeling the feeling but letting it go, until this becomes a matter of habit and we are re-programmed not to crave. But why should liberation not be possible at other points? And does it follow from the practical usefulness of this technique that we can give up craving altogether?

The first of these questions was asked by the off-beat English Theravadin monk, Ñanavira Thera[24]. Influenced by Existentialist philosophy, Ñanavira objected to the

---

[24] See Ñanavira Thera, Clearing the Path Path Press, Columbo 1987

apparent determinism of the remainder of the cycle – for it seems that, once you have allowed craving to creep in, you are stuck with the whole ensuing cycle of karmic effects from it and can do nothing about it. Human freedom does seem to make it possible that we could break the links at other points: for example, we could avoid contact with pleasant or painful things in the first place, or we could avoid grasping them once we have craved them.

Traditional Buddhism denies that these actions would have any spiritual efficacy, as they would not change our underlying tendencies. However, this seems to condemn the merely self-controlled to a life of unfulfilled craving. For example, if a habitual shoplifter gets the craving to steal something, but succeeds in resisting it and does not actually do so, has he not contributed towards future improvement of his habits at all? It seems that traditional Buddhism should at least be less dogmatic on this point.

The bigger issue here, though, is the second one. From the fact that craving can be prevented from arising, it does not follow either that it is always desirable to stop it, or that to be completely purified of craving would be the ideal human state. This has already been discussed to some extent in chapter 1. It may be that the most desirable state is not a complete purification of all craving, but a state of balance in which the worst effects of craving are contained.

After the discussion of rebirth in the previous chapter, it should also be clear that the move from craving objects in our normal experience in the present life phase to craving a new life in the future life phase is a gross over-extension of the psychological insights to be found in the present life phase. From the fact that we shape our lives through craving and determine many (though not all) conditions that subsequently affect us, it does not follow that craving makes our lives occur in the first place. Rather than being drawn to live again because of attachment to living, it seems just as likely that we are thrust into the world without prior motives.

The general principle of dependent origination

The general principle of dependent origination is found in several places in the Pali Canon:
> *This being, that becomes, from the arising of this, that arises; this not*

becoming, that does not become; from the ceasing of this, that ceases[25].

In other words, things cause and condition one another into existing in the form they take. If the conditions on which a thing depends cease, then so does that thing. This is supposed to be the nearest to ultimate truth one can get in verbal form, described, for example by Sangharakshita, as "the essence of enlightenment"[26].

It is certainly hard to contradict. In claims that seem obvious, though, it is hard not to suspect pseudo-profundity. So it is with this statement. Buddhists say that it is easy to understand in theory, but hard to really accept in practice. However, when one looks more closely at not just what it means in theory, but what it might mean in practice, it turns out not to mean very much.

We observe things conditioning each other all around us all the time. Caterpillars turn into chrysalises then butterflies: without the caterpillar there would be no butterfly. Without adding milk, your coffee will taste

---

[25] For example, this is found in the Culasakuludayi Sutta (section 7), Sutta 79 of the Majjhima Nikaya
[26] Sangharakshita, *A Survey of Buddhism* Tharpa 1987, p.108 ff.

bitter. If you keep eating lots of fast food you will put on weight. It could hardly be claimed that even small children do not appreciate the existence of conditionality. In fact, according to the philosopher Kant, we can't really make sense of things without it. We see the world through the spectacles of causes and conditions, so we can hardly help drawing causal and conditional conclusions about things all the time.

However, if dependent origination means this, then it can hardly be a difficult truth which is hard to put into practice. We are all putting it into practice all the time regardless of our degree of enlightenment or otherwise. So we must dismiss this interpretation.

If dependent origination is not something we take for granted already, then perhaps it must refer to a standpoint only accessible to the enlightened. Perhaps it is talking about things that *really* are, and thus are beyond our experience. Such claims about ultimate reality raise hosts of philosophical problems, but we do not need to tackle them yet (see chapter 7), because this interpretation of dependent origination just wouldn't make sense in any case. Ultimately real things are by definition *not* conditioned, and in any case the Buddha would be talking about something entirely beyond our experience that we could never grasp.

There's one other possibility: that the principle is not a general principle at all, but is actually referring to some specific conditions which we need to grasp and understand in order to make spiritual progress. Obviously some of these would be ones spelled out in the twelve links, such as the relationship between feeling and craving. If that's what Buddhism really means by this teaching, though, it's being put in an extremely confusing and unhelpful way. We don't need to know about *general* conditions at all, only about specific ones. We don't generally have a problem with acknowledging the existence of conditions in general, only specific conditions that we might have a problem with, such as the bad effects of habits we don't want to give up.

So, once more, Buddhism is its own worst enemy. It is claimed that we are confused and unenlightened through not understanding this law of conditionality: but actually it seems that we do not understand it for the more prosaic reason that it is not clear. There may well be conditions that we need to understand, but they are not in any way expressed by this. Presumably it is the urge to metaphysics which is again getting in our way. The Buddha had some very useful practical instructions about specific conditionings to offer to his disciples, but either he or they couldn't resist turning this into a metaphysical "truth" about the nature of the universe.

Mutual causality and interdependency

A possibly slightly more useful interpretation of dependent origination is offered by the modern American Buddhist teacher, Joanna Macy[27]. She suggests that dependent origination should be interpreted in terms of mutual causality instead of linear causality. Whilst in traditional Western thought we tend to assume a model of causality in which separate individual events lead to other events, the alternative view, now being used particularly by systems theory, is to think of the universe as consisting of interrelating systems which continue to influence each other over time. So, for example, if you were studying the relationship between an animal and the plant that it habitually eats over time, it would not be very useful to try to break

---

[27] See Joanna Macy, *Mutual Causality in Buddhism and General Systems Theory*, State University of New York Press, 1991

down your understanding into individual plants causing specific changes for individual animals and vice-versa: rather the system of the animal species and the system of the plant species interacted *as a whole*. The beaks of some species of hummingbird are precisely adapted to access one particular type of flower, from which it takes nectar and spreads pollen. The flower, however, is also adapted specifically to be accessible only to that species of hummingbird. It is impossible to say which caused the other in individual terms, so it may be more helpful to think in terms of the mutual adjustment of systems.

This interpretation fits with a long tradition of stressing interdependency in Buddhism. The image of Indra's Net, in which every node connects with every other node, for some sums up what they see as the truth in dependent origination: that no object exists separately, but only in dependence upon other objects. The spiritual significance of this is that we have a tendency to think of objects in isolation from each other, and have a distorted understanding of the world around us created by greed and hatred. A separately existent object is much easier to possess or to reject than one which is acknowledged to be part of a complex system.

If we think of dependent origination in this way, then it becomes an extension of the doctrines of impermanence and insubstantiality (anatta), discussed in chapter 1. Anatta is useful in pointing out that we mentally construct the objects around us as being a certain way, rather than knowing that they actually are like that. Impermanence also has the merit of pointing out that what we assume to be the continued existence of things is also a construction of our own. Interpreted in this way, dependent origination points out that objects may not exist *independently* in the way we often assume they do, but only in relation to other objects.

As I pointed out in chapter 1, however, the insights to be found in these doctrines remain useful only insofar as they are not taken to be metaphysical truths about either the real world, or even the phenomenal world. We simply do not know whether there is anything independent in the universe, or that we always make the spiritual mistake of thinking of things as independent when they are actually interdependent. It seems quite possible that we could also make the reverse mistake, of assuming that things are interdependent when they are actually independent. To take a simple example, a jealous wife might assume that there is an interdependent relationship between her husband's absences on business and the simultaneous absences of an attractive female friend. To get over her irrational jealousy she might need to appreciate that these absences are coincidental, not interdependent in the way that she had been assuming.

It is clearly the case that quite often by recognising interdependency we can gain more control over greed and hatred. For example, by recognising that a piece of meat has an interdependent relationship with an animal and an exploitative farming industry rather than just being a piece of meat from the supermarket, I might overcome the desire for meat with all its negative effects. However, it is not necessarily the case that we gain control over greed or hatred in this way, because we could also have greed or hatred towards objects recognised as interdependent. Someone venting their spleen against "the government" for example, will not necessarily be stopped by it being pointed out that the government is interdependent with the voters, the taxpayers, the civil service and international organisations. The negative feelings towards the government are perhaps just as likely to spread out contagiously towards everything else it touches, possibly extending to everyone and everything. The relationship between that negative feeling and the exact way its object is conceived is contingent.

So it is quite often useful to think of things as related by mutual causality and as interdependent. However, this is very far from being a profound truth about the universe that we should all learn to appreciate in order to be enlightened. For one thing, we do not know that it is always true, and for another, spiritually useful overcoming of illusions does not always coincide with a realisation of interdependency or of mutual causality. The reverse is quite possible: I might get over my illusions about someone by thinking of them as independent rather than interdependent, for example seeing a particular civil servant as an individual person rather than part of a vast (and faceless) interdependent system of government that I might resent.

Once again, a potentially useful practical point applicable to some situations has been overextended and made misleading by being turned into universal metaphysics. One can only conclude from this section and the previous one that, contrary to many Buddhist claims, *pratitysamutpada* is far from being the central insightful principal of Buddhist teaching it is often claimed to be. Where it appears to be insightful, this is only insofar as an overextended principle happens to coincide with our experience. The central principle should not be seen as a metaphysical principle, but rather one that provides an overall method for interpreting experience – the Middle Way.

Chapter 6: The trouble with Reality

In several of the chapters so far, I have already discussed some of the drawbacks of basing Buddhism on metaphysics. At the centre of these drawbacks is the idea that Buddhism is about breaking through to *Reality*. Note the capital "R" here, which distinguishes metaphysical talk about Reality from other uses of the word in everyday conversation. Talk of Reality with a big "R" involves misleading claims which, though they may seem abstract and irrelevant to some, are the basis of other mistaken thinking in Buddhism that does make a big practical difference. Talk of reality with a small "r", however is just a common way of talking about conditions that we need to face up to (e.g. "She just won't face up to reality", meaning that she is not addressing some important conditions).

To get to grips with what is problematic about Buddhist ideas of "Reality" it is necessary to do some critical metaphysics. However, the goal of this endeavour is ultimately practical. Critical metaphysics is metaphysical discussion engaged with in order to help get rid of metaphysics, rather as a trainee doctor studies diseases with the goal of eradicating them. It may sometimes take a practised eye to distinguish critical metaphysics from dogmatic metaphysics, just as some cures superficially resemble the diseases they tackle, but the intention behind the two types of metaphysical discussion is quite different.

What is even more confusing is that Buddhism contains both critical metaphysics and dogmatic metaphysics. This chapter attempts to unravel them a little more.

It's all in the mind

Some years ago, I attended an academic conference of British philosophers. At that time, I was less doubtful than I am now about using the term "Buddhist" to describe myself, but to openly confess to being a Buddhist amongst analytic philosophers was often a complete conversation stopper. Eventually I started to have a conversation with one philosopher who was at least mildly interested in the fact that I was a Buddhist. I tried to explain some of the key practical points of what I thought Buddhism was about.

"So how," he then asked, "do you reconcile all that with the belief that the universe doesn't really exist?"

I don't think I gave a particularly coherent reply, as I was rather surprised to find out that I didn't believe that the universe really existed, and that it was taken for granted by Western philosophers that this is what Buddhists believed. At the time I thought he had got it wrong, but over time it's become clearer to me that this idea hasn't reached common belief out of nowhere. It is indeed an aspect of what Buddhists commonly assume.

The view that the universe doesn't really exist is called idealism. Buddhism is idealist in the sense that it believes that all our everyday experience is based on delusion. Those who gain enlightenment learn to pierce this delusion and understand things as they really are, but in the meantime, due to our delusion (and the greed and hatred it gives rise to) we are affected by Reality without really understanding it. Thus Buddhism is idealist as far as the unenlightened are concerned, but realist as far as the enlightened are concerned.

Another way of putting this is to claim that conditioned existence is delusory, because it is only the product of changing conditions which we grasp only with a deluded mind. However, in traditional Buddhist teaching there is a further Reality beyond this which is not conditioned in the same way:

> *There is, monks, an unborn, and unbecome, an unmade, and uncompounded; if monks, there were not here this unborn, unbecome, unmade, uncompounded, there would not here be an escape from the born, the become, the made, the compounded*[28]. (Udana 8)

The idealism in relation to the unenlightened here depends on the realism in relation to the enlightened and vice-versa. We are only supposed to be able to recognise that we experience an unreal universe because there are those who have experienced the real one and who can make a comparison. However, belief that there are or have been such people (the enlightened) and that they have experienced the real depends purely on faith, as I have already argued in chapter 2. This claim about an ultimate reality is no less remote and unprovable for us than, say, the claim that God made the universe.

---

[28] Udana 8

In a universe in which 99.99% (or more) of the inhabitants are deluded, there is also no way of telling whether those who claim to have experienced reality are not deluded as well, but have just experienced another type of delusion or another level of delusion. If they are wrong, the whole idea of unreality collapses because there is no measure of reality to compare it with. The idea of basing a standard of reality on so few people is comparable, say, to calling everyone else "stupid" because one in a billion has an IQ over 200, and having an IQ over 200 is the only basis for not being stupid. This means that even highly intelligent people would be "stupid", just as, according to traditional Buddhism, many extremely wise people are still living in an unreal fantasy-world.

The drawbacks of this approach are obvious. The type of delusion that Buddhism is concerned with is that of not recognising and responding adequately to conditions, which is something we fail to do to varying degrees. Delusion lies on a continuum, yet enlightenment is apparently an all or nothing affair. It has to be an all or nothing affair so long as it is linked with the belief that the enlightened get to understand Reality. Reality is an all or nothing affair, as you either understand it or you don't: anyone who hasn't got there yet may be wrong.

Once again, Buddhists have weighed themselves down with metaphysical baggage that is completely unnecessary. If we saw reality as a continuum rather than as absolute Reality, and the understanding of it as also a continuum, the model of spiritual progress in Buddhism could accord much more closely to people's experience.

To do this would not mean giving up on there *being* a Reality. Perhaps there is, or perhaps there are just endless layers of interpretation and differing types of experience: we don't know. What we experience is delusion, which we become aware of when our assumptions are proved false by subsequent events: we do not experience Reality. To be able to unpeel layers of delusion does not require knowledge of Reality, only a careful interpretation of our experience. If we are honest, then, we should give up all pretensions not just to direct knowledge of Reality, but also to indirect knowledge through the appeal to the enlightened.

To do this would mean not giving up any guarantees that existed before. Believing in a Reality, and believing that this Reality is communicated by the enlightened, does not give anyone a guarantee either that this belief is correct or that they have grasped the teachings of the enlightened correctly. So in dropping the pretension of Reality, no-one is left any more uncertain than they were before. Relative experience always had to be the basis of judgement in any case, as this is all we ever have to go on.

Buddhism without an appeal to Reality would not be getting lost in nihilism. It would not lose its basis for objective values, because these were always based on relative progress known through experience in any case. Instead it would be returning to the Middle Way, away from the eternalist appeal to an absolute metaphysical Truth.

Buddhism without an appeal to Reality would also no longer be idealist, because its idealism regarding the unenlightened, as I noted above, depends on its realism regarding the enlightened. If you accept the implications of the admission that there may only be a continuum of reality, then we are also no longer condemned to Delusion as an inevitable fixture until we are enlightened, only to delusion as a relative experience. The universe we experience is not necessarily unreal.

This also seems by far the most sensible way to interpret the world around us. As I look out of the window as I write this, there is a young olive tree, glistening in the sunlight and swaying slightly in the breeze. Is it not likely that there is in fact an olive tree there? Granted that my view of the olive tree is partial, and that there will always be some degree of doubt about it, nevertheless, there being a real olive tree there, rather than an illusory one that is only in my mind seems by far the most plausible interpretation of my consistent experience of it.

The emptiness of the emptiness of emptiness

However, the argument in part a is based only on the early Buddhist and Theravada view of enlightenment. Mahayana Buddhists are likely to complain that Buddhism has already long since seen through all these problems with the metaphysics of Reality, and adapted accordingly. Some points that relate to the mainstream Mahayana will be discussed in this section, and the different approach of Zen Buddhism in the next one.

There have been lengthy metaphysical disputes about Reality within the Buddhist tradition, for example between the Sarvastivada school which believed in ultimately real phenomenal entities, and the Madhyamaka school which denied that there were any real entities. However, these opposed schools were only arguing about how the process of delusion should be explained – is it that we put together things that are actually there wrongly, or is it that there is nothing there in the first place? The central idealist belief – that when we look at something in front of us (say, a tree) what we think is there is not really there – remains.

The Madhyamaka school (led by Nagarjuna) also put forward a critical metaphysics, a development of the Middle Way, to show how our experiences are neither true nor false. Potentially this is neither idealist nor realist, but asserts that Reality is beyond all description. This philosophical perspective is linked to the practices and texts of the Perfection of Wisdom, where this critique of metaphysics even becomes the basis of a meditation practice, the contemplation of emptiness. "Emptiness" basically means the constructedness and ultimate unreality of all the concepts we use, and naturally this extends also to the concept of Emptiness itself. The contemplation of emptiness culminates in the emptiness of emptiness.

The Madhyamaka critique of metaphysics seems to confirm a lot of the points I was making in the previous section – except that Buddhists rarely see it that way. Instead of giving up the concepts of enlightenment and Reality, the inspiration of the Madhyamaka seems to lead Buddhists only to reinforce them by finding increasingly subtle accounts of them. The Madhyamaka functions as a spoiler for radical criticism of Buddhism rather than as an inspiration for reform.

One of the ways that the Madhyamaka is made compatible with other Buddhist conceptual language is through a rigid distinction between ultimate metaphysical language and conventional language. Thus Buddhists will happily recite texts from the Perfection of Wisdom such as the Heart Sutra, which acknowledges that nirvana is a construction with no relationship to Reality, in the same ritual in which they express their aspiration for nirvana and appeal for the support of beings that have attained it. When questioned about this, they are likely to say that conventionally there is nirvana, even if ultimately there is no nirvana. We have no choice, short of nirvana, other than to express ourselves in conventional language.

This means that the effect of the (purely theoretical) acknowledgement of the Madhyamaka critique of metaphysics is to put all conventional language on the same level of acceptability. Instead of *applying* the Madhyamaka critique in order to throw themselves back on experience, and use experience as the basis of judgement, Buddhists habitually keep the Madhyamaka critique in a conceptual isolation where it can have no effect on the rest of their thinking. The emptiness of emptiness is not just empty because a further level of theoretical criticism can be applied to it, but also because it is completely abstracted and apparently has no further effect on those who contemplate it.

It may be objected that Mahayana Buddhists simply do not agree with my interpretation of the implications they ought to draw from Emptiness. The practical implication, they may say, is not to abandon conventional Buddhist beliefs, but just to hold them a little more lightly, with more provisionality. However, it is not possible to hold a metaphysical view provisionally. Provisionality requires the possibility of change when new experiences come along, but the belief in Reality is not based on experience, but only on faith reinforced by tradition that there is such a Reality.

The Perfection of Wisdom, and the Madhyamaka critique of metaphysics, is possibly the biggest philosophical spoiler in history. You may object to Plato's crypto-Fascist state, or Jesus' belief in the Last

Judgement, or Confucius' patriarchal conservatism – but at least with these thinkers you know what they stand for, and they do not pretend to also believe the opposite. In Mahayana Buddhism you may think you agree, or at least find a fruitful acceptance of mystery; but you do not really know what it stands for, or what else you may be unwittingly asked to swallow with your emptiness.

Reality is here and now

However, there is a third kind of approach to Reality found in the Buddhist tradition: that of Zen Buddhism, which is descended from the Tathagatagarbha school of Indian Mahayana Buddhism. Perhaps seeing some of the limitations of both early Buddhist and early Mahayana approaches I have discussed above, Zen contradicts, or transcends, both. Rather than seeing Reality as something accessible to us only in the future when we are enlightened, Zen says that Reality is here and now, in our experience, for we are already enlightened *now*.

This Zen approach does have the virtue of pointing us towards our experience. Unfortunately the underlying model of what we are seeking has not changed from other forms of Buddhism, only the model of how we are seeking it. We are still trying to gain "enlightenment", even if the Zen terms for enlightenment, such as *kensho*, often do not seem to refer to an achievement on the scale of the Buddha's. The idea is still to break through to a Reality which is different from the delusion we experience now. Even though on the Zen account, we can break through to that Reality suddenly and unexpectedly during our everyday lives, we still need to shift to a qualitatively different state to perceive that Reality.

If one could drop the language of enlightenment (or its lesser versions) from Zen, one could interpret it as talking about smashing through delusions. There may well be occasions when a delusion is dispelled suddenly, by an intuitive process, so that one experiences being on a new level. However, dogmatic metaphysics enters the frame whenever Zen assumes that there is anything final about this type of insight. This idea of finality might not just show itself in outwardly metaphysical language (which Zen generally tries to avoid), but also in the revelatory authority placed on the masters who have achieved it, or in a neglect of the aspects of spiritual life which require a more gradualist approach, such as ethics (for Zen is effectively forced to deny the possibility of moral progress).

Zen has a discontinuous model of spiritual progress, which might fit with some aspects of experience, but certainly conflicts with other aspects. Its simplicity and directness have often appealed to Westerners, but as with the Madhyamaka, the apparently critical stance towards metaphysics functions more as a spoiler than as a stimulus for applying a critical perspective (rather than just a mysterious paradoxicality) to the assumptions that are still being made, and which still underlie the social and moral structure of Zen. It is a matter of course in Zen to deny that there is any path or any goal, but this functions in a similar way to the absolute sayings in the Madhyamaka, that are not taken seriously at a conventional level. It is better to affirm that there is indeed a path and a goal, in terms that can possibly be related to our experience, than to compensate for the abstraction of metaphysics by playing paradoxical games with it. It is not Reality, but reality, which is here and now.

Quantum irrelevancies

Before leaving the topic of Buddhist views of Reality, I would also like to briefly look at two perspectives that have influenced some Western Buddhists, and which they have tried to incorporate into Buddhism to varying extents: these are quantum physics, which I will look at in this section, and Deep Green philosophy, which I will look at in the next. In both these cases, Buddhists appear to have seized upon what they see as alternative "Realities" from Western culture, which they believe can be used to challenge more common Western assumptions about Reality, and show that the Buddha Really did see things as they Really are.

Quantum physics has indeed set some puzzles for those who think they know what Reality is really like. Together with Einstein's Special Theory of Relativity, it has challenged the belief of earlier Newtonian physicists in an orderly and predictable universe made of bits of identifiable matter. Quantum physics has shown that many of the regular physical laws that apply to the everyday world we normally observe do not apply at the level of sub-atomic particles.

Sub-atomic particles, such as electrons, do not behave in the predictable ways, following predictable laws, that larger bodies seem to follow. Their behaviour, far from being predictable, can only have a probability placed on it. It is also difficult to pin down exactly what a sub-atomic particle *is*: since we cannot observe it directly and its behaviour is irregular, it is difficult to decide whether it is matter or energy.

The underlying philosophical issue that creates this effect seems to be the effect of the observer on the observation. If I was observing the track of a planet in the sky, I could be pretty certain that my observation is not going to affect what the planet is doing; but if I "observe" a sub-atomic particle, the only ways in which I can gain information about its behaviour is by interfering with it in ways that compromise the neutrality of my observation.

If there is any lesson to be learned from this relevant to the spiritual life, it would appear to be one about the effects of the mind on observation. Instead of this, some Buddhists[29] have foolishly pounced on quantum physics as evidence about the universe itself: that Reality is insubstantial in the ways claimed by Buddhist tradition (for example in the First Noble Truth, or in the

---

[29] This is a widespread view, but for one expression of it see the website www.quantumbuddhism.com

Madhyamaka doctrine of Emptiness). Quantum physics is sometimes believed to undermine the materialism of the classical scientific approach, with the idea that materialism (the belief that everything in the universe is made out of matter) is a type of delusion of moral and spiritual significance.

All of this, though, is completely irrelevant. Quantum physics may cast doubt on some previously-held views about material reality, but it does not tell us anything at all about Reality. Quantum particles may or may not turn out to be substantial in some way, we just don't know. The idea that the conclusions of quantum physicists are final is just as misleading as the belief that the Buddha's achievement was final.

In addition, even if the quantum physicists had discovered something definite about the non-existence of substantial matter in the basement of the universe, this would in itself be of no spiritual or moral relevance whatsoever. It would not, at a practical level, change anyone's desire to possess things and make them part of their egos. Ice cream tastes the same whether it is ultimately made of matter or made of energy. Although (in my experience) Buddhists frequently confuse the "materialism" of believing that the universe is made of matter and the "materialism" of wanting to possess material things, there is no necessary connection between them at all.

In many ways this debate reflects the debate about the Sarvastivada in early Buddhism, and is equally useless. The Sarvastivada thought that objects were built up from actually existent phenomenal particles, whilst others such as the Madhyamaka denied this. However, this made no difference to anyone's practice in overcoming craving when their craving was stopping them from addressing conditions, as one way of overcoming craving might be to recognise that the thing you are craving is insubstantial, and another that it is made up of small particles. There may also be many other possible techniques for overcoming craving. There is no reason why one of these strategies should be more likely to be successful than the other, as all that is actually required is a different standpoint on the object of experience to gain some leverage on one's delusions about it. One doesn't have to know what it ultimately is, or is not, to do this. Similarly, one does not have to have any positive view on whether there is substantial matter at the root of things to use any kind of reflection on other ways of looking at it to undermine one's delusions about it.

Nugatory nature

Finally, I would like to comment on another modern view of Reality that has been recruited to the Buddhist metaphysical cause: the belief in Nature. In some ways it is understandable that people should turn to this view today, as the potentially disastrous effects of human action on the environment have become ever clearer. We have been neglecting some important conditions in our environment, and it is tempting to conceptualise this neglect as a neglect of "Nature". For many Western Buddhists, sympathetic to the Green movement, "Nature" is another way of talking about the Reality experienced by the enlightened, a Reality of interdependence, which we have ignored because of our delusion. The temptation to think in this way, I would argue, should be firmly resisted.

The reason for this is that "Nature" is such an ambiguous and manipulable term that its use invariably leads us into all kinds of assumptions which lie far beyond experience. It often vaguely refers to the environment beyond human control, including animals, plants, weather and landscape. However, there is nothing very much left on earth which has not been influenced by humans in some way, so we end up picking and choosing some kinds of non-human phenomenon as "natural" and others as "unnatural". Bare hills denuded by sheep, for example, are not at all natural in the sense of untouched by human activity, so why is it "unnatural" to erect wind turbines on them?

The word 'nature' is also frequently used to refer to human activities that are more traditional or culturally sanctioned. Farming is seen as a more "natural" activity than manufacturing plastics, but there is really no consistent basis on which to support this. Homophobes tend to see homosexuality as "unnatural" only because they do not see it as a proper part of their human culture or tradition.

The only thing that seems to be consistent in the use of "Nature" is that it is good, and approved by the speaker, but apart from this we will habitually describe as "natural" whatever we happen to approve of, picking and choosing between the different vague senses in which the word is used. In effect the word means nothing, because it means everything. It certainly does not refer to any Reality, only to a bunch of human delusions about what they think lies beyond them.

There is also nothing that can be consistently described as "natural" phenomena beyond, if not our manipulation, then at least our interpretation: even distant stars are understood only in a framework that we have provided. Nature does not exist.

So, one can go even further in criticising Buddhist attachment to this idea than in criticism of the belief that the enlightened have encountered Reality. Not only do we not know that there is such a thing, and not only is it counter-productive to hold such beliefs, but we do not even have any consistent way of talking about it. It is vital to address environmental issues, but in a way that helps us to overcome the delusions we have in relation to the environment rather than compounding them. To that end I suggest that whenever Buddhists (or others) are tempted to use the word "nature" they stop and think about what conditions they actually mean, and talk about those instead. For example, the effects of pollution are not due to 'nature' paying us back for our abuse of the earth's resources, but they do indicate conditions that we failed to address when we used those resources.

The uselessness of attaching nature-talk to talk about interdependence should also be clear from chapter 5. Interdependence as a general principle tells us nothing specific about the kinds of conditions we need to address. There are some specific conditions that we should recognise more fully as essential to our lives: for example, complex eco-systems and water cycles. However, there are also some specific conditions that we may need to worry about a little less than we do, such as economic conditions. Identifying "Nature" with interdependency tells us nothing about how to get to grips with conditions, but rather diverts us from the specific environmental problems that demand our attention.

Chapter 7: Buddha Trouble

In this chapter I want to discuss the role of the Buddha-figure in Buddhism, whether as a statue or just as an idea. The Buddha is a symbol of the attainment of enlightenment. However, before I discuss the Buddha-figure specifically, it's important to look first at the role of symbol and ritual in general. I am not going to dismiss symbol or ritual in a dry rationalistic fashion, but neither does that mean that symbols and rituals should be exempt from critical assessment.

Symbol and ritual

Throughout the Buddhist world there are Buddha-statues in all kinds of styles. There are also stupas, mandalas, lotuses, and (in the Mahayana) numerous variant Buddhas, bodhisattvas, and other symbolic figures. These figures are focuses and emblems of Buddhism as a religion, and they are also objects of worship, from a simple bow to an elaborate ritual lasting several hours. What is the point of all this?

Most Buddhists will explain that Buddhist symbols and rituals are reminders of their ideals, reminders of their commitment to those ideals, and motivators at a profound level which appeal to their aesthetic sense and power their emotions towards the ideal. Buddhist symbols and ritual help to develop saddha (faith), in which the heart is directed towards a higher Reality. It is not enough just to have an intellectual idea of Buddhist ideals and practices, they may say: we also need to work at an emotional level. Public Buddha-figures and collective worship also helps to bring the *sangha* (community) together with a shared sense of purpose[30].

This is the theory, but what is the experience? My own experience of about 20 years of varying levels of participation in Buddhist rituals is that they have only rarely had the intended effect. It is true that I have sometimes had a positive aesthetic response to the Buddha figure, or to the whole shrine on which it is set – but no greater than my aesthetic response to other things, such as works of art or landscape. Having shared symbols, and participating in ritual, may also at times have helped to make me feel part of a community; but more often I have felt alienated and oppressed by the collective aspect of ritual. Once the novelty had worn off, habituation to symbols and rituals

---

[30] For more of these kinds of explanations, see Sangharakshita, *Ritual and Devotion in Buddhism*, Windhorse 1995

created a regular response of boredom and alienation. Often I tried to ride through this, or accepted people's assurances that if I just kept doing it I would reach a breakthrough. Occasionally, indeed, I have had unexpectedly positive experiences of ritual, but the general pattern is that the longer I did it, the less meaningful it became.

Of course, my own response is conditioned by my particular temperament. However, I have heard many other Western Buddhists confess to alienation from ritual. Very often their motive for continuing was simply faith that if this was what prescribed by a religion with so many other positive things in it, then it must be useful in the end. Of course, some people appear to take to it readily and enjoy every minute of it, but amongst those who are practising Western Buddhism there is at the very least a large minority, possibly even a majority, who are to some degree alienated from it. This is not counting those (probably many) who have been put off from being involved further in Buddhism *because* of the symbols and rituals, and have then voted with their feet.

This is not because symbol and ritual is, in principle, a bad idea. Symbols and rituals are quite a basic part of the human condition. In most households you will probably find a mantelpiece, or some other place, where the values of the household are symbolised, whether individually or collectively. If we did not have Buddha-figures we would probably have fine-art prints, or rock'n'roll memorabilia, or tasteless ornaments. Ritual, whether individual or collective, is just a further extension of this kind of value-symbolisation. Rituals may help us focus our energies, adapt to changes, or simply feel part of a caring community. Even those of us who don't feel the need for regular religious ritual will usually participate in weddings, funerals, family gatherings, or farewells for colleagues at work.

No, the problems with Buddhist symbol and ritual seem to be related, like most of the other problems in Buddhism, to dogmatic metaphysics. Because the tradition is associated with revelatory authority, people go along with the forms of ritual associated with the past, rather than designing new rituals which are better suited to the needs of the present context. People try to engage with the symbols and the rituals because they are part of the tradition, but they are deracinated, having little connection with their culture or the rest of their lives. This makes it very much harder for the symbols and rituals to be successful in their supposed function of inspiring a positive emotional response.

Dogmatic metaphysics also comes into play to make this situation worse in common Buddhist response to this situation. Because of Buddhist idealism for the unenlightened, and the tendency to believe that it is the individual's mind that should be adapted to the circumstances rather than the other way round, most complaints about symbols and rituals will be met with an assurance that one should persevere and work at adapting oneself to them in order to get the benefits. No-one, generally, thinks about adapting the symbols and rituals to the needs of the participants, or if they do so it is in a rather marginal way, tweaking the traditional forms rather than designing new symbols and rituals from the beginning.

Then, a more profound problem lies in the symbols and rituals themselves. As I have been indicating, for example, in relation to symbols of love in Buddhism in chapter 3, Buddhist symbols tend to be symbols not of the path but of its goal; they are idealisations rather than symbols of the experience of spiritual progress; they symbolise metaphysical absolutes rather than aspects of human experience. I have already mentioned the thousand-armed

Avalokiteshvara as a particularly grotesque example of this, but even the simple Buddha-figure itself is often an idealised figure (I will come back to this point in the next section). Not only Western Buddhists, but even traditional Buddhists in Eastern countries might benefit from an overhaul of Buddhist symbols which addressed this question.

The theoretical purpose of symbol and ritual in Buddhism is laudable. People need symbols. However, they need symbols which reflect their aspirations, and that they can whole-heartedly respond to. In collective settings people also need symbols which are open to a wide range of people and are not alien to the audience. Finally, people also need symbols which help them progress in the right way and in the right direction, rather than just encouraging attachment to a metaphysical idea. For most people in the West, current Buddhist symbols are not doing any of these things, and it is not sufficient for a minority to respond that the symbols work for them, unless they want Western Buddhism to degenerate into an esoteric cult for a few people, something like the Rosicrucians. Much more radical thinking is needed about symbols without delay.

Warts and topknots

The Buddha-figure is familiar, not only to every Buddhist, but to a large number of other people as well. It is simply the figure of a man, usually seated cross-legged, but sometimes standing or lying. Both the artistic style and the features of the figure vary enormously depending on the origin of the figure, from Japan to Sri Lanka or perhaps from a Western artist. Formally speaking, what makes such a figure a Buddha-figure, as opposed to a figure of any other man, is its possession of the traditional thirty-two marks of a great being. The most frequently visible and distinctive of these are long earlobes, some sort of topknot, and what usually appears to be a wart above the bridge of the nose, in the centre of the forehead – which is intended to represent the "third eye" of wisdom.

However, what usually draws Western people to the Buddha figure is his expression: calm, subtlety and elevation emanate from a well-made Buddha figure. In this sense the Buddha-figure is like any other sculpture, which may provide strong aesthetic inspiration, part of which is created by the achievements of the artistic tradition in which the Buddha is made. However, not every Buddha figure does this just because it is a Buddha figure conforming to the traditional norms. Some traditional Buddha figures obey all the rules but are distinctly uninspiring (though of course this is a matter of taste).

Whether the Buddha-figure relates to your experience, then, depends on a number of factors: not only the artistic skill of the maker, but your own understanding of the tradition in which it is made, your ability to appreciate art, and the placing of the Buddha as a symbolic object worthy of worship. It also depends on whether the Buddha represents qualities that you can relate to your experience. Does it just stand for a metaphysical abstraction of enlightenment, or does it represent qualities that inspire spiritual progress from the place you are now?

The answer seems to depend on how far the artist has succeeded in representing spiritual qualities from experience, and how receptive you can be to the qualities the artist has represented. It does not depend on the formal marks of a Buddha, such as the wart and topknot. It is the warts and topknots that stand for the metaphysical dogma in people's relationship to the Buddha, because they have been put there only in obedience to tradition, and to mark out the figure as an enlightened figure.

The expression of the Buddha can model spiritual qualities and inspire spiritual effort, whether or not its qualities are supposed to come from an enlightened being. Other sculptures could also inspire such qualities. However, there are some good reasons for continuing to use Buddhas rather than other sculptures. The artistic tradition of Buddha-making is not just a tradition of dogma, but also a tradition of skill. There is not necessarily anything dogmatic about choosing to limit artistic expression to particular traditional forms. The dogma emerges when the traditional forms are all there really is to the piece.

As noted in relation to ritual in the previous section, there will always be some individuals who relate to symbols of enlightenment readily enough, and will be able to project their experience onto a form that represents an absolute. However, there is no reason why the rest of us, that are not able to do this, should find ourselves bowing to Buddhas that do not, in fact, represent any particular spiritual quality but rather only a metaphysical abstraction. Nor is there any reason why the only figures bowed to or worshipped should be Buddhas with warts and topknots. For example, if a reproduction of Michelangelo's *David* or a Greek statue of Apollo fulfilled the same function, there is no reason why these should not be used instead.

Buddhists may respond here that the purpose of Buddha-images is not only to inspire spiritual qualities, but also to represent the historical Buddha, and the enlightenment he achieved. For Theravadins at least, the Buddha-figure reminds Buddhists of the fact that a human being was able to reach enlightenment, as well as the qualities of the Buddha. Of course, there is nothing wrong with representing a historical human being, but if the meaning of the representation is so dependent on beliefs in Reality and revelation, we have again struck the rock of dogma. Since the capacity of human beings to make spiritual progress is in any case not in the least dependent on this supposed historical achievement, it is probably more useful for Buddhists *not* to be reminded of such claims. If that is what Buddha-figures really represent, perhaps modern Buddhists really would be better off with statues of Apollo, as in that case it would be clearer to them that the figure is only symbolic of spiritual qualities, and no other dogmatic claims come into play.

In general, though, there is no reason why all kinds of people, Buddhists or not, should not be inspired by figures that happen to have warts and topknots, nor why they should not cultivate and express that inspiration in any way they wish, whether bowing, prostrating, or whatever. It is attachment to the warts and topknots as ends in themselves that seems to be problematic.

Buddha gone baroque

In the Mahayana we have a broader picture as regards the role of the Buddha-figure. In Tibetan Buddhism particularly, but also in other forms of Mahayana Buddhism, a rich and complex set of variants on the Buddha-figure emerges. There are a huge variety of figures representing different aspects of enlightenment, including Avalokiteshvara and Tara representing compassion, Manjushri representing wisdom, Vajrapani representing energy, and Vajrasattva representing purity. The Five-Buddha mandala offers a whole system of symbolism where Buddhas symbolising different qualities are associated with colours, directions, animals, and other associated symbols. Not limited to Buddhas, Tibetan Buddhism also offers bodhisattvas, female deities, wrathful deities, protectors, dakinis and more.

This symbolic system is not only found in Tibetan and other Mahayana art, but also in the meditation practices in which these symbolic figures are visualised, known as *sadhanas*. Indeed, it is claimed that the artistic representations derive from meditation experiences, rather than the other way round. The variety of figures symbolic of enlightenment may be stimulated by meditation, or in turn stimulate meditation experience. It may be engaged in at a shallow level by the mere viewer of art, or at a deeper level by the meditator.

This incredible wealth of symbology can be overwhelming, and it is easy to be either overawed or repelled by it. However, it seems to be subject to exactly the same kinds of factors as the simple Buddha-figure of Theravada Buddhism. In some respects this rich symbolism may relate to our experience and provide spiritual inspiration, but in others it may also just express a commitment to a fixed idea of transcendent enlightenment which does not speak to our experience. We need to consider how the artistic tradition is being used, as well as our degree of cultural access to it.

Just as real spiritual qualities can be conveyed through the expression of a Buddha-figure, so they can also be conveyed (especially to someone instructed in the symbolic system) through colour and symbolic association. By this means an aesthetic rather than intellectual way is found of conveying a spiritual quality which can be dwelt on, whether through visualisation, or producing or appreciating art, and with enough dedicated practice this may help the practitioner to make that quality a habitual part of his or her response to the world. For example, a Buddhist who meditates on Tara, the female figure representing compassion, may develop an aesthetic and symbolic correlate for compassion, which only needs to be recalled to stimulate a compassionate response. I have come across an example of this recently in the travel writing of a Buddhist friend. In the middle of a threatening situation in which he was beginning to feel intense fear,

> And then, as if receiving a blessing, the mantra of Green Tara, Buddhist goddess of compassion who protects from fear, arose in the depths of my mind and something in me relaxed. Perhaps the moment of death was approaching, here in the dark Sri Lankan jungle. Some part of me accepted this, I felt incredibly aware and alive. The mantra continued to

sound without any conscious effort on my part. Time slowed to moments of prolonged intensity[31].

However, my friend's experience is exceptional, and I wonder how often the theory of symbolic correlation actually reaches fruition in practice. For it to work in this way, a number of conditions need to be in place. The meditator needs to have a dedicated and consistent practice over a period of time, a strong visual imagination, and a strong cultural access to the Mahayana symbolic tradition. Even for those who have a dedicated practice and a strong visual imagination, for Westerners the third condition – cultural access to Mahayana symbols – is very difficult to acquire, and might still be deracinated even after decades of practice. The cultural forms we are exposed to in childhood seem to have a very strong conditioning effect, which means that it is very difficult to gain such a deep engagement as is required here with an alien cultural form. For someone brought up in a culture saturated by Christian or secular types of artistic endeavour, understanding of other types of art or symbolism tends to be shallow and intellectual. Other forms may be attractive, but only superficially.

---

[31] Rijumati, *Pilgrimage to Anywhere* chapter 3 (unpublished manuscript)

Even when these kinds of obstacles are overcome by long immersion in traditional Buddhist cultural forms, there are further problems. The complex symbolism of, say, Tibetan art can very easily become an end in itself, and the authority of tradition given to it may well mean that all it comes to represent for the viewer is a metaphysical absolute which just becomes a matter of attachment and leads nowhere else. This might particularly be the case when one has committed oneself to the Buddhist tradition, but the branch of it that one is committed to regards engagement in all these symbolic forms as a necessary and non-negotiable part of Buddhist practice. It seems likely that this is the case in most Tibetan Buddhist groups, and I have also found it to be so with the FWBO, which makes much use of the Tibetan figures, though often in slightly modified forms.

In the FWBO, in theory one could ignore it and concentrate on other aspects of Buddhism, but in practice it is impossible to ignore if one wants to be part of the group, because of its widespread use in collective ritual. When the shrine hall is hung with pictures of Padmasambhava, Avalokiteshvara etc, and collective worship is frequently devoted to them, they hardly become an optional aspect of the group's practice. This means that for many, there is also likely to be a cultural resistance to these forms, which interferes with the spiritual benefits they could gain from other aspects of the group's practice.

The test of whether these many forms of the Buddha are really being used only for spiritual inspiration, or whether they are primarily to reinforce group-values, create commitment to a metaphysical absolute or have just become an end in themselves, is how far they are contingent. Could they be replaced by other symbols which do the same job, even if those symbols do not originate in the Buddhist tradition? Or could the figures be modified, even removing what tradition may dictate to be their "essential" features, in order to do their job better in a Western context? If the very idea of this is inconceivable, I would suggest that the main function of the figures is in fact the perpetuation of dogma and narrow attachment, not spiritual development.

Westerners attempting to use the Tibetan symbolic system as a spiritual tool have the odds stacked against them so much in so many ways, that at the very least I would suggest that it be regarded much more as a pursuit for highly committed (and self-selected) enthusiasts only, rather than standard fare for the mainstream of Western Buddhists. This is not at all to reject symbolism as such, or to reject the idea of symbolic systems such as those used by Tibetan Buddhists. However, new, or very much more radically modified symbolism would be far more successful. More than anything else, also, renewed symbols should represent not enlightenment as it is said to be achieved, but rather the process of moving forward from our current experience. This probably means that the mere recourse to symbolism needs to be supplemented with more expressive or realist types of artistic expression as they are found in the Western tradition, and that the kinds of symbology that can be used need to be understood much more flexibly.

What would this actually mean? Well, imagine you walk into a Buddhist shrine-room one day in the future, and a ritual for the inspiration of compassion is about to begin. On the shrine is not a Buddha or a Tara figure, but a realistic painting of an old woman. The participants have spent some preparatory time working out what would symbolise compassion in their experience, and have brought in a number of smaller pictures. Poems are read, songs are sung, symbolic objects are placed on the shrine, most of them Western in origin and originating from the immediate environment, although one or two people include Buddhist, Christian or even Hindu pictures which speak to their experience.

What would be Buddhist about this? Nothing needs to be except the overall intention and the underlying framework of the Middle Way. By celebrating compassion, the people are focusing on one aspect of conditions which we all need to address. Certainly in doing this, they need a clear intention, and they need concrete forms to relate to, rather than just abstract ideas. However, the assumption that the concrete forms will be more successful just because they are ones approved by traditional Buddhism is one that is in conflict with central Buddhist insights.

Mandalas and lotuses

It is not only Buddha-figures that are used in the Buddhist tradition to symbolise spiritual aspirations. Clearly there is something about a representation of another human being that has a powerful effect on other human beings, but more abstract representations are also used to represent spiritual aspirations. I think very similar questions can be asked about these to those I have asked about Buddhas. There are three types of symbols I will consider here: mandalas, stupas and lotuses.

Mandalas

Mandalas are circular diagrammatic representations of enlightenment, which allow the different elements of enlightenment to be shown in a spatial relationship to one another. The centre of the mandala represents the ultimate union of spiritual qualities, whilst each section of the circle can represent different constituent elements of that union. The distance from the centre can also represent the relative importance of the elements to the final union, with less important things towards the outside and more important things closer in.

The basic idea of the mandala is hugely flexible, and it also has the great virtue of showing incremental relationships through the spatial relationships of the diagram. The unifying point is traditionally taken to represent enlightenment, but it can also be taken to represent a psychic integration in which conflicting elements of the conscious and unconscious mind are unified. For this reason it was much admired and used by Jung, in a way which was not specific to the

Buddhist tradition[32]. Jung even thought of mandalas as universal symbols found in all unconscious minds, and distinguished them in dreams. In one of Jung's own recorded dreams, a city is laid out like a mandala, but the centre of his energies is experienced as an illuminated island in the centre of the city[33].

Mandalas are therefore one symbol of the Buddhist tradition that seem to clearly relate to universal experience, and offer little possibility of being turned into mere metaphysics. The mere fact that they show relationships places them within the realm of experience. It might be a good idea for Buddhists to follow Jung's lead by making fuller use of mandalas, which are only encountered occasionally at present. However, the limitation of mandalas is obviously that they are relatively abstract, and thus lack the emotional power that might be experienced in a Buddha figure. The combining of mandalas with figures, as in the Five-Buddha mandala, might be one way of

---

[32] See C.G. Jung, "Concerning Mandala Symbolism", from *The Archetypes and the Collective Unconscious* Routledge 1968
[33] C.G. Jung *Memories, Dreams, Reflections,* Flamingo 1983, p.223-4

addressing this limitation[34]. Again the fact that the different Buddhas in the five-Buddha mandala are placed in a symbolic *relationship* to each other makes them harder to interpret in a purely metaphysical sense, for metaphysics is about absolutes rather than relationships.

Stupas

Stupas are encountered throughout the Buddhist world in many different architectural styles, but they are basically pointy monuments in which the point represents enlightenment. In some ways they are like mandalas in three dimensions, and some great Buddhist monuments (like Borobodur in Indonesia for example) combine stupas with a mandala arrangement. However, the different dimensions outward from the point of a stupa are rarely differentiated: instead the monument is hierarchical, with the different levels of the monument being used to symbolically represent the path upwards to enlightenment.

A meditation practice called the stupa visualisation illustrates this structure by getting the meditator to build up a visual image of a stupa in the mind's eye. The

---

[34] For more on the Five-Buddha Mandala, see Vessantara, *Meeting the Buddhas* Windhorse 1993, part 2

stupa is built up of different shapes which are also different colours, and represent a hierarchy of elements, working up from the most basic (earth) to the most refined (consciousness). The visualised stupa can also be used to reflect on the relationships of each of these elements to one's own being, as one ascends from the lowliest elements to the most refined[35].

This hierarchisation of elements does seem to show a particular set of relationships in experience, but imposes a rather rigid structure on those relationships. There are hierarchies in our lives: for example a hierarchy of needs, or a hierarchy of states of consciousness in meditation. In such hierarchies, the higher levels are built on the lower ones and depend on them for their continued sustenance. However, the idea that spiritual progress is arranged in vertical layers is a metaphor which can easily be imposed too rigidly on our experience. To think of the "more subtle" mind as higher than the gross body, is a rather misleading idea found in some Buddhist scriptures (such as the Agañña Sutta[36] in the Pali Canon), which could distract us from the ways in

---

[35] For more on the stupa visualisation see Kamalashila, *Meditation: The Buddhist Way of Tranquillity and Insight*, Windhorse 1992, p.227-9
[36] Digha Nikaya sutta 27

which the conditions of both body and mind need to be addressed. When we get to the top of the stupa, we still need to carry on maintaining the bottom layer.

The stupa originated as a funereal monument for the Buddha's mortal remains, and stupas continue to be used in this way, as grave monuments, particularly for great Buddhist teachers. For this reason there are many customs adhering to stupas, such as the idea that you should only walk around them clockwise. Seen in this kind of way, stupas seem to be much more merely monuments to the exceptional metaphysical status of the enlightened or the spiritually advanced, and the customs surrounding them often become a matter of group conformity, of little real spiritual significance.

The usefulness of stupas as symbols of spiritual inspiration thus seems to be limited, but again this will vary between individuals and different cultural settings. They can certainly be used to symbolise one aspect of our experience of spiritual progress, but the cultural rules surrounding the circumambulation of stupas, and the exaggerated respect often accorded to them by Buddhists often also smell of metaphysics.

Lotuses

Finally, the lotus is another frequently used symbol for spiritual awakening. Unlike the mandala and stupa, it is not at all diagrammatic, but is rather an organic image that evokes the idea of the unfolding of potential in the spiritual life. The significance of the lotus, which is a type of water-lily, is also based on the idea that, like enlightenment, the lotus is pure, even though it grows out of the mud of unenlightened existence.

The idea of the purity represented by the lotus strikes me as not at all helpful as a symbol of the spiritual life. If the lotus grows out of the mud it has a close relationship to the mud, and its "purity" is just a metaphysical abstraction which has been associated with the aesthetic feelings evoked by the beauty of the lotus. One can admire this beauty without needing to feel that it is "pure".

On the other hand, the ways in which the lotus can be used to symbolise the experience of unfolding potential seems very positive. In this respect, however, the lotus is not different from any other flower, or indeed any other growing organism. Lotuses have been hugely over-used in Buddhist scripture and symbology, and are also very specifically Indian, and do not grow in more temperate climates. It might be better to make full use of the symbolic power of other unfolding flowers, as celebrated by many poets, if it is unfoldment that we wish to celebrate. In doing this we could also move beyond the metaphysical connotations and the cultural limitations of the lotus.

Chapter 8: Dharma trouble

The word "Dharma" in Buddhism can be translated "Law"," Truth", "Religion", or "Doctrine", and it means all of these things. In fact, the Dharma is simultaneously believed to be a universal truth that is eternally present, and the teaching of the Buddha or his followers, and any other true teaching. To Westerners bored with the precise distinctions of Western science or philosophy, this might seem enticingly ambiguous. However, it is also a recipe for confusion and a dangerous use of language. If you want people to believe what you say without critical examination, one way of doing so is to lead them to think that by definition it's the truth – and if the word you use for truth is the same as the word you use for your doctrines, this is quite an easy slippage to fall into.

In this chapter I'm going to look in a bit more detail at the pros and cons of the different senses of Dharma and the ways they can be confused: first at the universal and particular senses of Dharma, then at the associated issue of relationships between Buddhism and other religions.

Wasn't it true all the time?

The Buddha's Dharma is often said to be eternal, meaning the Buddha just happened to discover it in this age, but it was there anyway for anyone to discover. It will also still be there in future, ready for anyone to discover, even if it has died out in the meantime. Anyone could also discover the Dharma by themselves, without contact with Buddhism, and even in theory become enlightened all by themselves (becoming a *pratyekabuddha*).

This universality of the Dharma is something that always appealed to me. It is what led me to think that there is nothing Eastern about Buddhism, and any culture through which Buddhism has expressed itself is entirely accidental. If we take it seriously, not only can Buddhism be completely (not just partially) Western, but the Dharma can even be seen completely independent of Buddhism, perhaps even being practised in the cultural context of other religions. Indeed, if Buddhism is supposed to reflect and support the Dharma, it should be completely flexible in its acceptance of that Dharma wherever it is found.

But do Buddhists take the universality of the Dharma seriously? They may pay lip-service to the idea of Dharma being everywhere. They may even describe a certain non-Buddhist book or film which seems to capture important insights as "dharmic". They may even make a distinction between "dharmic" and "Buddhist". However, the "dharmic" is there to provide extra spiritual snack-food, not to be invited into the Buddhist feast. No matter how closely their ideas and inspirations may cohere with those of the Buddha, no one is accounted a Buddhist who is not a follower of the Buddha. "After all," they may say, "Isn't that what Buddhist means?"

A parallel could be made here with scientific theory. A credible scientific theory should be one which is fruitful in predicting events which may confirm or deny it. It does not matter who or what is the originator of a scientific theory, only what relationship it has with evidence. Scientific theory, of course, is not exactly the same as Dharma, but aspires to universality in the same way. Excluding pieces of Dharma as "Not Buddhist", however, is akin to, say, excluding scientific theories because they were formulated by people who were not English-speakers.

The measure for Dharma should not be "Is it Buddhist?" but "Does it fit with the core insights of Buddhism?" The fact that the core insights of Buddhism are not universally understood in the same way by all Buddhists perhaps provides a practical reason as to why Buddhists have fallen back on purely cultural criteria, but it provides no excuse for doing so. Rather, it provides a reason for urgently clarifying the core principles (as you will have seen in the earlier chapters, I think this means giving precedence to the Middle Way as the only truly universal doctrine in Buddhism). Only once the principles have been established can the Dharma then be discriminated with more confidence.

In the Western Buddhist Order I used to find a large measure of agreement that the Dharma was universal, could be distinguished from Buddhism, and was based on principles. Unfortunately, though, when it came to making important judgements about what was a right doctrine, these points were insufficient. This was partly because tradition still competed with principle for precedence, as the traditions were still vaguely believed to embody the principles when this was not necessarily the case. It was also partly because the principles themselves were not clear. Instead of the Middle Way, the two most commonly cited were dependent origination (*pratityasamutpada*) and Going For Refuge to the Three Jewels. I have already discussed the former (see Chapter 5), which is useless as a general principle because it implies nothing specific. Going For Refuge to the Three Jewels (Buddha, Dharma and Sangha) is a faith-practice found throughout Buddhism. It is often interpreted as beginning with faith in the Buddha's enlightenment, immediately defining Buddhism in metaphysical terms: but even if it is interpreted more liberally than this, it is a very culturally Buddhist construction, and hardly a starting point for identifying the universal Dharma.

Sangharakshita, the founder of the Western Buddhist Order, in the important task of trying to develop a "Western" (or genuinely universal) Dharma, seems to have left the job half-done, and thus left a muddle behind him in which no-one is really sure what the universal principles are, and the ones given do not have clear practical applicability. This may simply be because, due to his conservative tendencies, he was unwilling to clearly put the universal Dharma first and use it to resolve all other ambiguities in the tradition.

The prioritisation and clarification of the universal Dharma is the most important task facing Western Buddhists today. It is theoretically recognised by Buddhists that the Dharma was there all the time, but that the Buddha just happened to be one bloke who found it, but this point does not seem to be given nearly the emphasis it deserves. Certainly its implication that the Buddha is entirely dispensible needs to be more widely drawn. The universality of the Dharma is also incompatible with the notion that belief in the Buddha's enlightenment is essential for spiritual progress, which simply has to be dumped if you believe that the Dharma is universal. There is nothing holy or mystical about this self-contradiction and confusion: rather it stands in the way of spiritual progress.

Putting it in context

Apart from the universal law or truth, the other aspect of the traditional Dharma is the teachings given in specific times and places, by the Buddha and by other great teachers of the Buddhist tradition. These teachings are often believed, to a greater or lesser extent, to be a result of the *skilful means* of the enlightened, being exactly the right words that needed to be uttered to a particular person, in a particular context, at a particular time. This skilful means is particularly stressed in the Mahayana as part of the training of the bodhisattva, a being dedicated to saving all other beings who should thus be truly flexible in the way he/she communicates. Among engineers, the bodhisattva will speak the language of engineers; among Muslims, the language of Muslims, etc.

Skilful means can otherwise be thought of as the skill of education, and involves bringing down the universal Dharma to a level of particularity. It is very obviously sound. If people are to benefit from Buddhist teachings and practices, they need to hear them in a language they will understand. What would be rather odd, though, is if a particular example of the contextual Dharma were to be taken out of its context and represent the universal Dharma. Supposing the Buddha had talked to a convention of engineers and explained the Middle Way to them in terms of weight-bearing ratios, then for ever afterwards, whenever the Middle Way was mentioned, it could not be done in any other way than in terms of weight-bearing ratios. This would seem rather odd, but it is exactly what has happened in a good deal of the Buddhist tradition: specific contextual manifestations of the Dharma have been confused with the universal Dharma.

The largest contextual manifestation of the Dharma is that of the Buddha himself. He appeared in a specific context (northern India) and a specific time (approximately 500 BCE). All the teachings he is recorded as giving should thus be treated as contextual Dharma directed to the people of that time and place, unless we can also find genuinely universal teachings (such as that of the Middle Way) amongst them. However, the default position should not be (as many Buddhists seem to assume) that the Buddha's teachings are to be treated as universal until shown to be contextual: instead, they should be assumed to be contextual until proven universal. Of course the Buddha will have been addressing particular people with words that related to their circumstances, but these words may or may not be relevant to ours at all. To be relevant to our time his words need both to be justifiable, and to imply other points that would impact on our practice and experience in our own context.

Of course, just because a piece of Dharma is contextual rather than universal does not mean that we have nothing to learn from it: but it does mean that we are in the position of overhearing a conversation that is intended for someone else. That other context may have concerns that overlap with our own as a matter of chance – but there is no reason to assume that it always will. This is why reading the Buddhist scriptures is largely an appropriate pursuit for an antiquary: from Buddhist scriptures we largely learn about other people's lives as we do from any other historical document, and it is only here and there that we can gather scraps that are either universal or coincident with our own context.

Even the style of the Buddhist scriptures derives from their use for another purpose than the one we use them for today. The scriptures of the Pali Canon were used for memorisation and chanting before being written down, so they are full of repetitions and memorable patterns: they were not produced for thoughtful individual reading at all. Even once you have got past the style, the remaining material often involves highly contextual discussions, which may be of historical or human interest, or show the Buddha as an inspiring figure. However, the content of the universal Dharma in the whole library of the Pali Canon could probably be summarised in a few pages at most. One has to pan a great deal of water to discover a few tiny nuggets of gold. To describe the Pali Canon as a whole as "Dharma" is a bit like describing the whole river Yukon as "gold" because those few tiny nuggets have been found in it.

We cannot create our own contextual Dharma simply by borrowing from someone else's contextual Dharma – or if we do, its truth will be a matter of accident. As argued earlier in the book, we also cannot justify contextual Dharma by anything other than universal Dharma, meaning a connection with the Middle Way, rather than appeal to tradition or to metaphysics. Teachings need to be derived from justified principles, not the other way round.

Note that I do not go to the post-modernist extreme of saying that all Dharma is contextual, or that all truth is context-dependent. The false assumption made by post-modernists here is that we are bound by the limitations of our language, which cannot describe any universal truth. If that language is restricted to principles about *method*, however, it *can* be universal in the same sense that scientific language can be universal: that is, interpretable (or discoverable) by all (even if it can also be misunderstood). Language cannot be universal and also try to represent a state of affairs, for the way we think things *are* is necessarily conditioned by our individual or cultural experience, and ever shifting.

Instead, the language of universal Dharma needs to be confined to the question of *how to approach and interpret* whatever we experience, so as to distinguish justified belief from falsehood. Inevitably, then, the language of universal Dharma will be a philosophical language. Such philosophical language is at least capable of its own type of justification – a universal practical objectivity.

Righteous Christians and holy Hindus

I shall now turn to another traditional aspect of Buddhist Dharma: the claim that Buddhism is, in some sense, *right*, and that other religions are wrong. Traditionally, Buddhists have a high regard for righteous Christians and holy Hindus, yet they would also have to say that their beliefs were mistaken in a way that even the most limited Buddhist ones were not.

This is one area where the Middle Way often gets a mention, with it being explained that Christians and Hindus, believing in the eternal soul, are *eternalists* whose beliefs, for that reason, are less useful in seeking enlightenment than those of Buddhists, whose beliefs follow the Middle Way.

Unfortunately, this way of interpreting the Middle Way is contextual, not universal, Dharma. In the Buddha's time, whether or not you believed in an eternal soul or self was of some importance in determining other beliefs and practices. Today, this pair of opposed beliefs are only two of many possible metaphysical positions to which one may become attached. The developments of Christianity, Islam, science, and 2500 years of Western philosophy since the time of the Buddha have made the debate very much wider.

A Christian or Hindu is, indeed, very likely to believe in an eternal self or soul, even today (though there are some Christians who rightly point out that belief in the soul came to Christianity from Greek philosophy, not from the Bible). They will also probably believe in the existence of God, and that an infinite, perfect God is nevertheless capable of taking the finite, human, form of an incarnation such as Jesus or Krishna. If one takes the Middle Way seriously, one needs to recognise that it may very well be the case that these metaphysical beliefs will prove an impediment even to the best of Christians and Hindus in grasping the truth beyond delusion.

But are these beliefs any more of an impediment than the corresponding Buddhist metaphysical ideas? Compare the Christian and Hindu beliefs with the Buddhist beliefs that the Buddha gained the most perfect state available to humans, and that this state gave him access to a truth beyond all delusion. The Buddhist beliefs here are just as far beyond experience. The claims for the Buddha's achievements may be more modest than those of God, but slightly smaller metaphysics is still just as metaphysical as big metaphysics. Smaller metaphysics is just as likely as big metaphysics to form the basis of dogmatic beliefs. If someone makes a claim on the basis that the Buddha experienced the truth of that claim in his enlightened state, that is just as dogmatic as claiming that God revealed truth to him, and in neither case is the claim then open to any re-evaluation on the basis of new evidence.

So, if the Middle Way is to be consistently and universally applied, Hindus and Christians are indeed mistaken in their eternalist beliefs, but no more mistaken than most Buddhists. This means that Buddhists really have no grounds to criticise their beliefs, for (at least without a better understanding of the Middle Way), they have no better alternative to offer in their place.

To look at this more positively, however, it is clear that we are all hampered by different metaphysical beliefs. Those who bear them should be objects of compassion rather than malice. Righteous Christians and holy Hindus are *no more* hampered by metaphysics than are good Buddhists. This should come as a relief to Buddhists who may have a real respect for their Christian neighbours, but struggle to reconcile this experience with a theoretical commitment to the idea that they are wrong (similarly to Christians who struggle to keep thinking that their kind, radiant Buddhist neighbours are going to Hell).

Traditional Buddhist claims to exclusivity of religious truth by appeal to a crude traditional form of the Middle Way, are completely incompatible with other traditional Buddhist truth-claims, which fall foul of the Middle Way as much as other religions do. It is only if Buddhists abandon many of these traditional positions that they begin to have any grounds to criticise righteous Christians and holy Hindus. However, in letting go of metaphysics they are far more likely to drop the criticism, recognising that metaphysics is a burden for all to work with, and the Middle Way in no way a "Buddhist" monopoly.

Oversold tolerance

Before I leave this chapter on Dharma, I'd like to also tackle another widespread piece of Buddhist exceptionalism: the idea that Buddhism is uniquely tolerant. As Sangharakshita claims:

> *Not a single page of Buddhist history has ever been lurid with the light of inquisitorial fires, or darkened with the smoke of heretic and heathen cities ablaze, or red with the blood of the guiltless victims of religious hatred. Like the Bodhisattva Manjushri, Buddhism wields only one sword, the Sword of Wisdom, and recognises only one enemy – Ignorance. That is the testimony of history, and is not to be gainsaid*[37].

Unfortunately the testimony of history is rarely so unequivocal, when viewed in a less partisan light. The Buddhist claim is usually that no war, or at least very few wars, have been fought *motivated by religion* in Buddhist lands. If one points out a few examples of Buddhist bellicosity, these are treated as exceptions to the general rule of Buddhist peacefulness. However, the evidence is that

---

[37] Sangharakshita, *Buddhism in the Modern World*

there has been no lack of wars in Buddhist lands, and whether or not a war is motivated by "religion" or "politics" is a question of highly subjective judgement.

Religious beliefs and practices can be closely associated with "political" wars, and politics is rarely absent from "religious" wars. Two examples of this are quite recent or current. One of these is the involvement of many Japanese Buddhists in their country's nationalistic expansionism at the time of the Second World War: Brian Victoria, in his book *Zen at War*[38] gives lots of evidence of Zen culpability. The other example is the intolerant Singhalese Buddhist nationalism in Sri Lanka, which has prevented a reasonable settlement to avoid thirty years of conflict with the Tamils.

Much evidence from further back in Buddhist history can also be found in Trevor Ling's book, *Buddhism, Imperialism and War*. Ling argues that although the stress on non-violence in Buddhism has resulted in more avoidance of confrontation in Buddhist South-East Asian society, this simply results in a suppression of aggression, which can be released firstly through gossip or other indirect means of intolerant communication,

---

[38] Brian Victoria, *Zen at War*, Weatherhill 1997

and secondly through war[39]. War in South-East Asia has also historically been without some of the constraints found in other cultures, and the complete lack of any tradition of Just War theory in traditional Buddhism means that the religion has done nothing to moderate barbaric killing when it breaks out. Instead, Ling shows evidence for the ways in which the monastic sangha in South-East Asia has been easily manipulated by kings to uncritically support nationalist wars.

The Buddhist claim to unique tolerance often in fact rests, not on Buddhist purity, but on an unfavourable comparison with Christianity – as in the quotation from Sangharakshita above. It would be hard to beat the united impact of the Inquisition, the Crusades, and the forced Christianisation of the Americas, so there is little doubt that Christianity (as a whole) indeed has a worse record on extreme violent intolerance than Buddhism. However, this is hardly a great achievement for Buddhism – a bit like being nicer than Hitler.

Another element of the argument usually involves a straightforward fallacy. Those Buddhists who have engaged in nasty wars

---

[39] Trevor Ling, *Buddhism, Imperialism and War*, Unwin 1979, chapter 6

and been intolerant of other religions or races are usually described as not acting according to true Buddhist principles. This confuses two definitions of "Buddhist": firstly those in the group who profess to be Buddhist, and secondly those who fulfil specific criteria for being a good Buddhist. If we only pick good Buddhists to count as "Buddhists" to start with, the result will be a foregone conclusion that Buddhists don't fight wars or behave intolerantly (just as it would similarly with good Christians), but if we count as "Buddhist" all those who profess to be so, it is far from the case that Buddhists have been exceptionally tolerant compared to other groups.

Finally, the exceptionalist Buddhist claim to tolerance may often involve a confusion of tolerance with passivity or patience. To be tolerant, one must have the power and the capacity to do something about what one doesn't like, but nevertheless choose to allow it. Merely putting up with something that one has no power over is not tolerance, nor is it tolerance if one is indifferent to it, and really doesn't care what others do. In areas where Buddhism has traditionally flourished at various times (such as India, South-East Asia, China and Japan), there is a cultural tendency to regard religion, not so much as an exclusive set of doctrines that one believes in, but as a set of available practices which one combines with others. In this kind of culture, people do not habitually do violence to each other on the basis of religious belief because they traditionally do not see religion as the kind of thing one fights about. There is little interest in religion as a single dominant commitment, and therefore little interest in getting other people to share that single commitment. People in these cultures have been predominantly either not interested in their neighbours having a single religious commitment like theirs, or have just been passive in relation to it, even if in some sense they would prefer everyone else to share the same allegiances.

The idea of tolerance was invented in Europe, and was the outcome of the Protestant Reformation and its attendant useless bloodshed. Those who began to practise tolerance then really did care about the other sides' beliefs – they strongly disapproved of them. They also often had the power to persecute religious minorities, but chose to grant them freedom of worship. Oddly enough, without experience of extreme conflict and intolerance, real tolerance could not follow. It is thus a mistake to attribute tolerance exclusively to Buddhism, or even a greater achievement in tolerance to the operation of its supposedly superior doctrines through history. It could be argued that Christian tolerance, purchased much more dearly and in knowledge of the effects of its opposite, is in fact much more valuable.

Whether the Buddhist doctrine of the Middle Way has a greater *potential* for promoting peace and tolerance in future, especially when united to the Christian tradition of tolerance which has developed into Western democracy, is another matter. It seems clear that it has exceptional potential to support tolerance, because all conflicts involve attachment to metaphysical views, whether these views are about politics, religion, necessary resources, or just the nature of the opponent. The more real practice of the Middle Way there is (whether or not it is done by Buddhists), the less attachment to those views there will be and thus the less likelihood of conflict. A real examination as to how much truth may be in an opponent's views, looking for the experience that lies behind them rather than just the metaphysics, also greatly increases awareness of an opponent and thus increases the likelihood of tolerance. However, the Middle Way is still largely untried. The Buddhist tradition has been so far adrift of it that it can hardly be said to have proved its efficacy in producing peace and tolerance one way or the other. Only future developments can potentially provide clear evidence in support of the practice of the Middle Way.

Chapter 9: Sangha trouble

The term "sangha" has been used in Buddhism both to refer to the community of monks and nuns, and to the wider community of all Buddhists. In either sense the Sangha is also traditionally the third of the Three Jewels, particularly reflecting the importance of social support for spiritual progress. In this chapter I shall be looking at a variety of issues concerning the social expression of Buddhism.

The trouble with monasticism

"Monasticism" is a general term for the ordination of monks and nuns as celibate spiritual specialists. To begin with the Buddha's ordination led to a wandering lifestyle, reliant on begging for alms, and only later did the order become "domesticated", settling down in fixed buildings. So, the crucial feature of monasticism is not the monastery, but the solemn commitment to the Buddhist path, with its disavowal of all former possessions and relationships, its celibacy, and its training in the Dharma through monastic rules (Vinaya). The solemn commitment is particularly symbolised by the wearing of robes, which set the monks and nuns immediately apart from the lay people.

Monasticism is still an accepted part of the vast majority of Buddhist schools today. Only the Pure Land and Nichiren sects in Japan have dispensed with it, together with the minority Nyingmapa School in Tibet, and more recently the FWBO/TBC , which I will return to in the next section. The most obvious advantage of monasticism is that of all specialisation: monks can concentrate on following the spiritual path whole-heartedly, without being distracted by other responsibilities. Buddhism also greatly appreciates the power of personal example, and the monastic system focuses on training the best men and women in the Dharma first, so that they will then be an example to everyone else.

However, given that monasticism is a social institution, it is important to consider it in its effects on society. The most important of these is that simply, in creating an elite group of spiritual specialists, one immediately condemns the remainder of the population to be spiritual second-raters. Like those who advocate selective grammar schools in English education, the advocates of monasticism too frequently focus on the advantages of selection for the elite, much less on the disadvantages of being denied such preferential opportunities to the remainder.

This does not mean that instead we should adopt some sort of egalitarian uniformity whereby nobody is allowed to benefit from talents, drives or creativity to access more resources that could be used to train him/her than those given to others. Rather, it means that we should not make fixed and long-lasting divisions in society that fix people's social roles, and deny some for the rest of their lives opportunities they might have benefited from. The monk-lay division is one such fixed division.

The consequences of that fixed division are those of high social status for the monk (usually less so for the nun) in Buddhist countries, constantly reinforced by rituals such as monks eating first and sitting above lay people. Such social status often renders real spiritual effort unnecessary, and makes the whole Buddhist religion primarily a matter of form: monks become more concerned with how they appear to lay people than with their actual spiritual state.

Striking evidence of the corruption of monasticism in the Theravada can be found in Sangharakshita's book *Forty-three years ago*, where he recounts some of his experiences as a Theravada monk in India. There apparently it was commonplace to engage in secret sexual activity, and even to have hidden families, but a bond of silence between the monks prevented this being made known to the lay people[40].

Perhaps we should not need such reports to expect the imperfection of monks in their role, only a fair knowledge of human nature as commonly experienced. Their role sets them up in an idealised position that often substitutes for the spiritual efforts of others, and that alone must cause a huge strain for many. Add to this the difficulties of celibacy (to which many Catholic priests have also proved inadequate) and you have a ready recipe for hypocrisy.

Contrast this with the situation of the lay people, who have to provide for the monks and nuns. Although in recent times the education of some lay-people has improved greatly, and lay-people may also be involved in what were formerly purely monastic activities like meditation and study, there are still all sorts of formal ways in which they are second class citizens of the Buddhist republic. In the Theravada they are still

---

[40] Sangharakshita, *Forty-three years ago: Reflections on my Bhikkhu Ordination*, Windhorse 1993

believed unable to attain enlightenment without ordaining first. Their goal is primarily a better rebirth, even in the Mahayana. Their prime virtue is generosity towards the monks, which is seen as an opportunity for the lay people to gain merit.

Generosity is indeed a virtue, but when such emphasis is put on it for one whole group in society towards another, one has grounds for suspicion. Suppose, for example, it was seen as the role of women to earn merit by being generous towards men, but men did not respond with material goods, only with good advice. It would be clearer in such a case that there was an unequal power relationship going on. Nor would men benefit in the long-run from not having to work to support themselves, any more than monks and nuns do. The loss of physical energy and initiative would be the most likely result, and this does seem observable in some Theravada monks – though of course there are many others who remain vigorous through practice, and Mahayana monks often have to work.

However, the deeper trouble with monasticism is not just to do with the power relationship involved and the lack of spiritual motives and opportunities for lay people. These factors do, in any case, vary a good deal through the Buddhist world. The deeper problem is due to the very model of enlightenment as the overcoming of desire that it rests on. The monastic system could never have been created by Buddhists who really had a transformational view of their desires rather than a purificatory one. If some of our desires have a tendency to produce suffering, the Middle Way solution, as I have discussed in earlier chapters, is not to pluck out or remove those desires, but to divert the energy they represent into better channels.

However, the monastic life is based on the removal or purification of desires: for example, celibacy is intended to stop sexual desire arising in the first place, and the rule about not eating after midday is intended to stop excessive desire for food. A transformational approach would be concerned, not with stopping these desires arising, but with balancing and integrating them. Sexual activity and food may be a source of healthy energy, and it is guiding and channelling these energies to stop them becoming obsessive or one-sided that is most important. Some people are able to use completely prohibitory practices for transformation with much effort and practice (for example, those who are celibate can succeed in channelling their sexual energy elsewhere), but this is so difficult that it can hardly be claimed to realistically be the main goal of the prohibitory practice. To re-channel a river, you do not dam it first and only then think about which direction to re-channel it, as the force builds up ready to break the dam. Rather, a genuinely transformational approach diverts the flow little by little to its new destination.

In the next chapter I will have more to say about the relationship of this problem to moral attitudes; for Buddhism as a whole is disadvantaged by the ethic of purity. The monastic system is a particularly strong instance of reliance on purity ideas. As we will see, purity has a close relationship with rigidity and rule-following, too, which is another feature of the monastic tradition.

Apart from the traditional monasticism that is still practised by many groups, I have noticed a sentimental attachment to monasticism even amongst Buddhists who do not practise it, such as the FWBO. This is because they still see the monastic life as an ideal model, even if they also feel that it cannot be feasibly practised in the modern West. I think it is this kind of underlying attachment to the monastic model that needs challenging most in the West. The Middle Way requires a focus on all conditions, not just temporary personal advantages. A monk or nun, through their status, is contributing to making a huge division in Buddhist society which is to the long-term benefit of neither ordained nor lay: for the lay-person needs the monk's training and refinement, whilst the monk needs the lay-person's energy and wealth. We all need all of these things without the influence of over-specialisation to prevent it.

The trouble with Orders

Given some of the above issues with monasticism, the approach of the FWBO (now Triratna Buddhist Community) has been to maintain the system of ordination, but to turn it into a system of non-monastic ordination. Members of the Western Buddhist Order are not necessarily celibate (only a very few adopt celibacy as an additional commitment), they do not wear robes, and do not follow monastic rules. They may continue engaged in "lay life", that is, jobs, marriages, children and mortgages. Their commitment is only to following the Buddhist path, not to a particular lifestyle.

I have personal experience of being a member of this Order, and I have little doubt that it is an improved model from the monastic one. Yet by the time I resigned from it, I had reached the conclusion that the underlying problem was not just monasticism, but ordination. Many of the underlying issues created by monastic ordination remained.

The biggest of these is the large social division created in the Buddhist community between the ordained and the non-ordained. In the FWBO a lot of store is set by ordination: a lot of time and energy goes into preparing for it, and it is granted, or perhaps lengthily deferred, by the preceptors. In some ways it may thus be harder work to become a member of the WBO than to become a monk. So admission to the Order becomes a badge of social status, a qualification, an entry to the elite – no less so because of the constant theoretical denial of this social significance, and the insistence that it is only a recognition of spiritual commitment and spiritual orientation. Like monks, Order Members are given a social status which they may then not deserve in some respects, even if they have worked hard for it in others, and the distrust shown to the uninitiated is suddenly turned into unreserved trust at the point of ordination.

As with the monastic system, the danger of complacency on the part of the ordained is matched by the opportunities denied to the non-ordained. However highly qualified, committed, or energetic they may be, the unordained meet constant barriers of trust and responsibility in the FWBO world that can be easily surmounted by the ordained. They cannot go on retreats that are limited to order members, where of course the most important discussions will occur. They often cannot sit on the trusts that make decisions for local FWBO groups. They have very limited opportunities for teaching the Dharma, even if they are highly skilled at it.

In short, the frequent complex and subtle assessments of the characters of others that we all need to engage in, in any organisation, are largely replaced by the one big formal discontinuous assessment of ordination. Once you are past this big test, you are likely to want to support the system that honoured you in that way, and before you pass it, your complaints will carry little weight. Our unbalanced development, our backsliding, and the limitations of preceptors' assessment abilities, cannot be taken into account by such a system. The same inequalities of power, regardless of skills, ability, or capacity for responsibility, are found here as in the monastic system; and, as in the monastic system, the ordained do not necessarily benefit from having unrealistic expectations placed upon them.

Defenders of ordination will say that it enables the FWBO to be in the hands of the spiritually committed, so that it will never be diverted from its most important spiritual goals, or taken over by those who do not understand them. However, this assumes that a picked elite group, well-versed in a particular set of cultural expectations that they have had to meet, is in a better position to judge the spiritual direction of a group than those who might bring in other ideas from outside. In effect, ordination ensures a degree of conservatism rather than encouraging the openness that might be required. It is not overwhelming commitment to a tradition that is required by the leaders of spiritual groups: it is freshness of vision, intellectual flexibility, and a realistic engagement with all conditions. I was disappointed in the extent to which I found these qualities in the Western Buddhist Order.

Defenders of ordination are also likely to say that it gives an overwhelming shape and commitment to an individual's life, which can transform it positively. The public role of the ordained is thought to be subordinate to the inner change, and to merely reflect it. In this case, then, the public role of the ordained, and the public ritual of ordination, becomes dispensible. Let individuals set themselves goals with great seriousness, and let their more experienced spiritual friends assist them in reaching those goals – long may this continue, but it has nothing to do with the social status of the ordained. If the individual process of working towards ordination is valuable for many (as it was, in some ways, for me), then let us simply take that process and decouple it from social status. Instead, spiritual progress should be its own reward.

The Buddhist Society of Friends

If Buddhists were to dispense both with monasticism and with any other kind of ordination, however, what should they put in its place? How else might the Buddhist community be organised? If it were ever to be organised in a radically different way, this should, of course, be on the basis on consultation and consensus. What I offer below is only a vision of how it could be done differently, not a rigid prescription.

Sangharakshita talks about the sangha as ideally a *community of individuals*, in which all participate freely, without any of the usual power mechanisms of groups. This was obviously his ideal in setting up the Western Buddhist Order. Yet there is a contradiction involved in setting up free community of individuals with a rigid boundary that has to be policed using power. Instead, the community needs to have graduated and near-invisible boundaries, which let in the maximum amount from outside that is compatible with the community maintaining its values.

There is already an alternative social model for a religious group along these lines to be found in the Western world, apparently flourishing, and having many values in common with those of Western Buddhists: that is the Religious Society of Friends, or Quakers. Of Christian origin but not exclusively Christian, Quakers meet weekly (or more often) in silent meetings, and conduct their business by consensus. As individuals, their beliefs vary greatly, but they are united by their meetings in the open, reflective power of silence. Only occasionally in their meetings there is "ministry", where one person feels inspired to make a contribution, offering their own insight for the moment.

Quakers have a membership, but they place very little emphasis on it, making most of their activities accessible to "attenders" (non-members who attend Quaker meetings) as much as to members of the society. In a

Quaker meeting, it is not at all obvious who is a member and who isn't. Some people speak in meetings who clearly have spiritual maturity and weight, yet there is no need for this to be formally marked by any special social status, ritual or clothes. In all things the starting point is simplicity.

What Quakers often seem to lack is spiritual techniques to give a bit more focus and dynamism to their calm, open gatherings, and these Buddhism offers in abundance. How wonderful if the richness of the Buddhist tradition could at some point be united with the simplicity, openness and unpretentiousness of the Quaker tradition! One could imagine silent meetings like those of the Quakers, but in which the "ministry" occasionally given was about the application of the Middle Way, or about personal insights recently reached. Such meetings could be supplemented by meditation instruction, but more formal ritual would be a private matter and a matter of taste, perhaps to be arranged between friends, not a public one. The Buddhist Society of Friends would have an understanding that ritual can be used as an instrument of social coercion, and its aim would be to get individuals to become freely involved at their own level without any such coercion. Anybody would be welcome, formally Buddhist or not, and attenders could engage in the society to a high level; but membership of the society would be based on clear commitment to the practice of the Middle Way as the most simple and overarching principle of Buddhism. Opinions on other aspects of Buddhist teaching might well vary, and might also be the object of lectures and discussions in the Society.

Like the Quakers, too, their openness of worship and accessibility need not preclude the Buddhist Society of Friends from involvement in social and political action. Meditation for them would not be an end in itself, but a way of working effectively with mental conditions. Action for charity and political campaigns might become just as much part of the total activities of the society.

Many Buddhists might respond to a proposal of this kind with concerns that without special ordained people to guard the central values of the community, they will be diluted and lost. This would tell us a lot about the conservatism behind much Buddhist thinking, and the tendency to think of the Dharma as the property of one tradition rather than something universally accessible. This conservative anxiety is misplaced, firstly because the Dharma will not be destroyed even if it is diluted by a particular organisation – it will always be there for people to discover; and secondly because the fortress mentality which accompanies orders, of "insiders" who can be trusted and "outsiders" who cannot, is antipathetic to the Dharma, and is far more likely to destroy it from within than any "invasion" or "dilution" of it from outside. It is time for Buddhists to open the doors of their hearts and of their organisations, and to count the risks of conservatism equally with those of the loss of the "Dharma" they hang onto so much.

Chapter 10: The ethics industry

Purge and purify

It often appears, to judge from the language used, that Buddhist ethics is understood primarily as a process of purification. For example, at the fortnightly *uposatha* ceremony undergone by monks, when the monastic rules have been recited, the leader asks "Are you all pure in this, brothers?" For another example, the Five Precepts, central to basic lay ethics throughout the Buddhist world, in the FWBO have a positive version:

With deeds of loving kindness, I purify my body.
With open-handed generosity, I purify my body.
With stillness, simplicity and contentment, I purify my body.
With truthful communication, I purify my speech.
With mindfulness clear and radiant, I purify my mind[41].

I have recited this formula probably thousands of times, and there must have

---

[41] The FWBO Puja Book, Windhorse 1990

been few of those, particularly later on, when I didn't wince at the endlessly repeated word "purify". It's such a relief now not to have to recite this any more, given that it's used as a reminder of basic group-identity, recited almost every time FWBO Buddhists come together.

Purity means a state of being without particular unwanted "pollutants", whether dirt, sex, unwanted people, wrong beliefs, wrong desires, or wrong actions. Purifying is a process of rejection, of getting rid of the unwanted. *Purification* is just the process of bringing about purity, so one can't engage in purification without at least implicitly thinking of purity as a desirable end.

If this is a metaphor, it's an extremely common metaphor, and it's one which seems entirely in conflict with the basic insights of Buddhism. The Buddha in attaining the Middle Way, did not purify himself of anything, but took the best from his previous experience and developed it. A person who overcomes anger in meditation, does not purify himself of the unwanted anger – any experienced meditator knows that to try to get rid of anger is only productive of more anger. An attitude of purification put into practice is very likely to lead to a negative attitude to the thing you want to purify yourself of, and to a destructive cycle in which one undesirable object is disposed of, only to be succeeded by another one popping up somewhere else – because the "pollutant" object has only been created by aversion, and if the aversion is still there, it will very likely just attach itself to a different object.

I've also been puzzled by the responses I have had from Buddhists when I point this out. They sometimes seem genuinely not to be aware that the formal Buddhist language they use is *riddled* with the idea of purity, and they deny that it exists. Or they may deny its importance. However, to deny the importance of language habitually used in a religious context is hardly in accordance with the Buddhist recognition of conditionality. The same people who may be very cautious about what novels and films they read or watch, for fear of their effects on their minds, seem quite happy to recite language, day in, day out, which is antipathetic to Buddhist insights.

Another kind of defence is the appeal to tradition. Perhaps this kind of language must be OK because it's been used for so long, or it goes back to the Buddha so it must be compatible with enlightenment. If this defence is used it becomes clear that the ethic of purification is another manifestation of attachment to metaphysics, and to the Buddha's enlightenment as a source of revelation.

Either way, this is another example of Buddhist tradition being its own worst enemy. Instead of helping people to actually understand the insights it has to offer, Buddhist ritual language cloaks it in something quite different which is very likely to give the casual onlooker a misleading impression. I know that Buddhist ethics, at their best, are about transforming the drive from one kind of unhelpful behaviour – violence, fraud, intoxication, or whatever – and turning it towards something positive instead. The actual process of doing this can be greatly aided by meditation. However if instead it is a question of *purifying* one's mind of violence, fraud etc. it has nothing new to add to the long tradition of ineffective prohibition to be found in the Abrahamic religions. Indeed, to see the full application of the purity ethic, turn to the Old Testament.

Memorise the regulations

Very similar issues apply to the other major source of moral guidance in traditional Buddhism – the *patimokkha* or monastic rules, which as I mentioned above should traditionally be recited fortnightly by a gathering of monks or nuns. Breaches of these rules should then be confessed to brothers or sisters in order to *purify* oneself and the community.

This tradition also shows the close relationship between purity beliefs and *legalism*. In order to purify oneself of a piece of wrong conduct, it must be closely defined, and its exact nature made clear so that all present can agree whether or not an offence has taken place. The monastic sangha at the uposatha gathering effectively becomes a court of canon law, with the difference only that for many minor offences, only a clear confession is needed and no punishment need be imposed. For major offences, however, a monk might be expelled from the sangha, or at least put out of communication with the other monks for a while.

Unfortunately, as too many leaders of institutions today (such as schools) still seem not to have grasped, legalism just does not work. If you define in precise language how people should not behave, and make them memorise and recite it, they are more likely to think about offending than they would otherwise, and are constantly put into a state of temptation by the reminders of how they might sin. They will also go to great lengths to find ways of sinning which are not technically in breach of the rules. The rules will then be modified to define the new offence as wrong too, and an endless process of rule, loophole, and hedge-rule will go on. Alternatively, they will obey the rules in form but not in spirit, and go about their activities in a spirit of constrained conformity but with creativity drained from their attitudes.

In the case of the monastic rules, large sections of the *Vinaya Pitaka* ("Book of the Discipline" of the Pali Canon) in effect show this process at work, as they consist in explanations of how a particular loophole in the rules was discovered and a new hedge-rule put into place to close the loophole. For example, monks are forbidden to engage in sexual activity or to be alone with women or to touch them. However, some monks started drawing rude pictures on the walls and claimed that this wasn't against the rules. Hence a new monastic rule had to be brought in against drawing rude pictures on the walls[42].

Whether this legalistic approach was necessary for the organisation of the

---

[42] Vinaya Pitaka, Khandaka, chapter 6

monastic sangha in the Buddha's time can be a matter of debate – perhaps it was. However, it is still a major part of the way in which ethics for monks are thought about today. What is the point of being a Buddhist monk if you have so little understanding of Buddhist ethics, or so little sympathy with its spirit, that you have to be controlled by sets of rules like little boys in a preparatory school?

Furthermore, scholarly discussion on Buddhist ethics in general frequently alludes to the Vinaya rules as though they were a major source of information on Buddhist ethics. In fact, though, they seem to be in major conflict with Buddhist ethics, given that Buddhist ethics begins with motives and states of mind, which are worked with to change behaviour. Buddhist ethics, apparently more than any other, must be concerned with the spirit of an action and whether that is relatively right or wrong, not with the letter. Letting the monastic rules speak for Buddhist ethics is a bit like letting the Pharisees stand in for Jesus.

One defence of monastic rules that might be given is the nature of their role in confession. Confession can be a heart-felt process in which a fault is recognised and fully acknowledged, so that one's resolve not to repeat it is strengthened. However, false or formalistic confession is the curse of legalistic religious organisations. There is no point in getting someone to confess something that they do not really recognise to be a fault, otherwise it just becomes an exercise in social regimentation. So, confession, if it is to work properly, should be of moral failures as spontaneously recognised by the person who confesses, not of a failure of adherence to a set of pre-defined rules. General principles might help one to reflect on areas that one needs to confess, but there has to be flexibility in the interpretation of these to meet the recognition that no formula ever fully captures moral conditions. Confession is an important, and potentially helpful, element of the Buddhist tradition, but it has no necessary relationship with the monastic rules.

In the end, then, the legalism of the monastic rules is inseparable from the whole question of monasticism discussed in the previous chapter. If monks and nuns are separated from lay people in this way, the need for accountability to lay people creates pressures for legalism in monastic life. The perfectionism of these rules then becomes a great burden of stress on monks, which they are unlikely to be able to fulfil, and provides more pressures towards hypocrisy or cynicism. Lay expectations are excessive partly because lay people can only vicariously lead the spiritual life through monks. The decay and misrepresentation of Buddhist ethics has thus been part and parcel of the monastic system, which in its turn was caused by an undue emphasis on purification rather than transformation in early Buddhism.

Follow the precepts

The ethic of purity does not stop with the monastic regulations, however. Exactly the same attitudes can be applied to the observation of the Five Precepts. In the FWBO there are also Ten Root Precepts taken by Order members which are just a slightly more detailed version of the Five, taking more account of mental states and different types of speech. Whether the Five or the Ten Precepts are used, they are sometimes treated just as a shorter, easier Vinaya.

Here are the Five Precepts in their more traditional negative form:

1. I undertake the training principle to refrain from striking living beings.

2. I undertake the training principle to refrain from taking the not-given.
3. I undertake the training principle to refrain from sexual misconduct.
4. I undertake the training principle to refrain from lying.
5. I undertake the training principle to refrain from intoxicants.

This list provides an excellent, though broad, summary of ways of behaving that are most likely to lead to bad consequences and create collisions with conditions around one. In this sense, provided their broad-brush nature is recognised, the precepts are a good application of the Middle Way. Other lists could be created, but this one does well in encouraging one to start to get to grips with conditions rather than living in a set of delusions[43].

Each of the precepts also contains the term "training principle" (a translation of the Pali *sikkhapadam*), which also suggests the provisionality of the principle, that you take it as part of a process of training. Unfortunately, though, this point is often ignored in practice. The recitation of this list

---

[43] For more precise information on how they might do this, see my thesis *A Buddhist theory of moral objectivity*, section 8.a.vi. This can be seen on the web at www.moralobjectivity.net/thesis8

in Pali also often means that many Buddhists recite in ignorance of exactly what they are reciting – they probably know the list of five things they should be avoiding in their own language, but are not conscious of the sense of "training principle".

Whether you think of these as generally ways of addressing conditions, or whether you think of them as a list of rules given by the Buddha, makes a big difference when it comes to interpreting what they actually mean in practice. In considering this one immediately enters a moral minefield of direct and indirect actions, definitions of the five things to be avoided, and exculpatory good intentions. Eating a bacon sandwich does not involve directly striking a living being, but some Buddhists would regard it as a gross breach of the first precept. Is viewing pornography on the internet a matter of sexual misconduct? This is a matter of definition. And what about lying for a benevolent reason, for example telling someone that you liked their present to make them (and you) feel better, even though it is untrue?

If you think of the precepts as basically rules, then you will presumably think that their interpretation is straightforward, and that there is no other possible interpretation than the one you take. However, there are a great many possible interpretations of the precepts – probably as many as there are people trying to follow the precepts. In my experience, this point often seems to be missed by Buddhist speakers who urge their audience to "Just follow the precepts!" The only possible outcome of treating the precepts legalistically is a false confidence in the unique rightness of one's own interpretation, which must also simultaneously condemn everyone else's interpretation to falsity.

If, on the other hand, you recognise that the precepts are not a set of rules, but rather a set of broad principles, and that their value comes not from an authoritative source, but rather in the extent to which they help people address conditions, you'll be in a much better position to make good use of the precepts. Recognising that they are only broad principles, though, simultaneously means recognising that they are not much use as guides to action. The precepts just do not give you any specific information on the rightness or wrongness of most of the things you might wonder about in the average day. Should I let my child play when she wants to and get on with her own thing, or am I neglecting her? Should I drive or cycle to the supermarket, given that I can carry more and save a lot of time if I drive? Should I have another cup of coffee? These three questions might conceivably be seen as related to precepts (the first, second and fifth respectively), but the precepts certainly don't tell me how to judge them in any sense.

To resolve issues like these, it is not the precepts but the Middle Way that can make the best way of judging clearer. The Middle Way provides a reminder to avoid fixed views and address neglected conditions. For example, I might recognise the anxiety about neglecting my child as just about social expectations, and conclude that there's nothing wrong in leaving her to play. That I really need to drive to the supermarket might also well be about a fixed view of how much time I can "afford" to spend on the operation, when cycling would address so many other conditions better such as the environment, fitness, setting the example to others and so on. Finally, I really shouldn't yield to the fixed idea that I need endless caffeine stimulation to operate effectively, but instead look at the long-term effects on mind and body – so no more coffee, thanks.

In the light of this I have often wondered at endless Buddhist emphasis on the precepts as the source of Buddhist ethics. They are useful in some ways, but in rather limited ways, and the much more useful Middle Way hardly gets a look-in where most discussions of Buddhist ethics are concerned. Most people most of the time are not contemplating murder, theft, rape, or fraud of a kind where the application of the precepts is very obvious, and 99% of the time we are in the much larger grey area where the precepts are ambiguous, and we need to work it out using the Middle Way as a guide.

If, as most Western Buddhists seem to claim, they do not treat the precepts as legalistic rules, then I think they need to start giving greater acknowledgement to their limitations as anything else, and certainly much more acknowledgement to the core Buddhist principle which does in fact offer moral differentiation of a more precise kind.

Skilful means

In the Mahayana, some of the limitations of the ethic of purity and of monastic legalism were recognised at an early stage. It could be said that an important part of the Mahayana revolt was an ethical one, for by the first century CE the monastic leaders of the Buddhist world were beginning to be seen as literalistic, narrow-minded, and individualistic.

The Mahayana answer to this was the Bodhisattva Ideal. The Bodhisattva is seen as a being who puts off individual enlightenment in order to save others, and is motivated by universal love. I have already discussed the effect of this ideal in chapter 3 in relation to the theme of love. However, another important dimension of it was the ethical approach represented by skilful means. The bodhisattva is not represented as a stickler for the rules, but rather as being willing to break them in a greater cause. In order to bring all beings to enlightenment, any rule could be broken. The end justifies the means.

As Damien Keown remarks, however, this alternative ethic has had a limited impact on the ethics of ordinary Mahayana practitioners[44]. It is normally seen as the skilful means *of the advanced bodhisattva*, meaning that it is only to be used by those with high levels of insight. So, whilst there are stories of bodhisattvas who kill, steal, eat meat, take intoxicants etc. because of their special knowledge that doing so would enable other beings to move towards enlightenment, beings without such knowledge are not entitled to use an

---

[44] See Damien Keown, *The Nature of Buddhist Ethics,* Macmillan 1992, chapter 6

intention to help other beings as an excuse for their bad actions. More ordinary Mahayana Buddhists are still stuck with the precepts and the Vinaya as prime Buddhist indicators of right moral conduct.

The effect of the skilful means doctrine, then, is not to liberate ordinary Buddhists from legalism, but to put them even more in the power of the revelations of the Buddha or other great teachers. Instead of encouraging ordinary Buddhists to integrate a concern for the consequences of their actions into everyday life, the doctrine of skilful means encourages them to feel themselves absolutely ignorant in comparison to great teachers, who understand so much that they are even able to bend the rules that ordinary mortals have to follow. Rather than encouraging us to see wisdom on a continuum, it separates people into the two categories of "wise" and "deluded" and reinforces the elitism already found in the monastic system.

The idea that it is leading beings to *enlightenment* that justifies the exercise of skilful means also takes it beyond the sphere of ordinary experience. Ordinary people are seen as too far from enlightenment to be able to judge what would reliably lead to this ultimate guaranteeing state. The more immediate development of wisdom, which ordinary people might better be able to see, is not taken to count as a justification for the exercise of skilful means. Thus the idea of an absolute goal and a final guarantee, which we have found distorting Buddhist understanding throughout, continue to do so at the point where Buddhist ethics show promising signs of coming out of their legalism. Because we do not have access to the revelation either of enlightenment itself or of (its substitute in the Mahayana) the experience of great beings who are close to enlightenment but are only putting off its final attainment, our judgement is, in effect, worth nothing, and we are enjoined to follow the rules.

At the very same time as figures like Nagarjuna were emphasising the Middle Way in Buddhist philosophy, Mahayana ethics were moving further away from it than ever. For the Buddha's approach to his own ethics involved questioning and experimenting with the words of the wise in his day, and questioning their assumptions in order to move beyond them. While still far from enlightenment, he was quite prepared to break the rules laid down for him by his father or by the ascetic tradition, using only his own limited and fallible judgement. For all the supposed rule-breaking in Mahayana scriptures, there is little sign of this kind of reasoned and experimental approach to conduct, but only big, sweeping revelations or their absence.

The academics move in

Finally, before I leave the topic of Buddhist ethics, it is important to mention another more recent phenomenon – the development of an academic "Buddhist Ethics" industry at a remove from the actual attempt to practise Buddhist ethics in experience. Some of the leading figures in this industry are not only not Buddhists, but are clearly not interested in any personal or practical side to Buddhist ethics which might make it important to develop practically justifiable moral ideas suited to the modern context. Instead their approach is to trawl the Buddhist scriptures and sociological observations of life in Buddhist countries to support an entirely descriptive ethics. So, you can read these authors if you want to know what the scriptures tell you about a certain moral issue, or what people do in Thailand in relation to it. But is it *right* to do what people do in Thailand, and if so, why? These academics will not help you with that at all.

It is Buddhists themselves who are to blame for this, by letting their own moral tradition dwindle into the irrelevancies of legalism, instead of developing richer and more practically useful accounts of how to go about making justifiable moral decisions. The academics, seeing a gap in the market for Buddhist ethical explanation, have sprung to fill it. However, they could only fill it from the distinctly limited moral ideas recognised by the tradition already, and have shown no interest in innovating.

The only solution to this is to develop an alternative account of Buddhist ethics based, not on scripture references and accounts of what people do in Thailand, but on the Middle Way. This approach should be able to tackle moral issues and, rather than calling in traditional Buddhist assumptions as metaphysical starting points, start anew with the avoidance of such metaphysics. For example, in discussing abortion, rather than starting (as many Buddhists do) with the belief that rebirth requires a foetus to be treated as a person, let us begin with what experience actually tells us about foetuses and try to avoid absolute assumptions either about them being persons or not being so. I have already written a book, *A New Buddhist Ethics*, which attempts this type of Middle Way account of Buddhist ethics, which is freely available on the internet (www.moralobjectivity.net/New_Buddhist_Ethics). I can only refer readers interested in further positive development of this topic to this source.

Chapter 11: The meditation bazaar

Meditation as an end in itself

Meditation is one of the three elements of the threefold Buddhist Path (together with morality and wisdom). It involves direct cultivation and training of mental states, whether through formal "sitting" or otherwise. It is probably the aspect of Buddhism that has had the most effect on the most people in the West, for not only Buddhists use Buddhist meditation techniques, but a wide range of other people use it for stress relief or other therapeutic purposes.

As a practice within Buddhism, however, it clearly does have a wider context and purpose and should not be an end in itself. The "inward" focus and reflection has the purpose of developing the whole character, affecting the "outward" actions of one's activity in the world generally. The withdrawal into meditation does not just have the goal of a pleasant inward experience, but is part of a difficult total transformation which also includes the examination of one's beliefs and actions from the bottom up.

This being the case, why have I nevertheless so often received the impression that, for many Buddhists, meditation *is* an end in itself?

Perhaps the strongest examples which appear to support this come from Tibetan Buddhism. Traditionally, some elderly Tibetan monks have had themselves walled into caves, with a chink to receive food, there to end their lives meditating. These monks can hardly have thought that the Path consisted of anything other than meditation, if that's all they had left to do. Even in the British Tibetan Buddhist community, there are three or four year meditation retreats[45]. A retreat of that length can hardly be aimed at integrating meditation with other aspects of the path – indeed many other aspects of the path must be forgotten altogether in the intense ascetic focus of such a retreat.

The Zen tradition goes in instead for marathon meditation sessions called *sesshins*. Here it is not even the quality of the meditation itself that seems to matter, but simply how great your endurance is at

---

[45] http://www.independent.co.uk/news/uk/buddhist-monks-seek-solace-in-a-retreat-from-the-modern-world-after-four-years-in-isolation-a-group-of-novices-at-europes-largest-tibetan-centre-emerged-to-face-some-familiar-prejudices-tim-kelsey-reports-1500974.html

continuing to sit. Even the Buddha is depicted as sitting down to meditate *until* he reaches enlightenment, no matter what. The assumption here seems to be that if you keep sitting and sitting and sitting, you must eventually reach a breakthrough – but intense physical discomfort and mental rebellion are far more likely, even for experienced meditators who go on for too long. As human beings we have limited powers of adaptability.

At a more personal level, my own experience of several retreats at Vajraloka, the FWBO's specialist meditation centre in Wales, was that the retreat leaders seemed to be trying to pack in as many hours of meditation as possible, no matter whether they were productive or integrated with the rest of the Path. Perhaps the most advanced meditators, like the most advanced musicians, after working up gradually over a long period of time, may manage to practise for up to eight hours a day. But to subject a group of no more than average meditators who have turned up for a retreat to such a programme seems crazy. And is meditating for eight hours a day really desirable, given the diminishing returns that are likely to follow from the extra time spent sitting?

Don't get me wrong here: I do think that meditation is an extremely useful thing to do. The world would be a better place if more people developed greater mindfulness, concentration, compassion and insight in the course of a daily meditation practice. Maintaining that daily meditation practice is also not at all easy, and any training we can get from more experienced meditators may be helpful with this. However, the value of meditation is the sort of value that only arises in a larger context, when the benefits of meditation are seen in daily life and help to transform one's approach to other activities. Someone who focused on meditation alone would be like an artist who painted a picture only containing reds and pinks, forgetting about the blues, yellows and other colours. Even if it was of predominantly red and pink objects, such a picture would lack depth and perspective because of its limited colour range.

Part of the reason why Buddhists may often treat meditation as an end in itself may be found, again, in the life of the Buddha. The Buddha is said to have gained enlightenment *in meditation*. He is described as gaining ever higher levels of *dhyana* (meditative absorption), before gaining enlightenment. It may be that enlightenment is for that reason seen basically as a meditative attainment, despite the distinction made in Buddhism between *dhyana* (meditative absorption) and *insight* (wisdom about ultimate reality), and the other ways of developing wisdom that exist outside meditation. This provides, then, another reason for not holding beliefs about enlightenment and not holding it as a goal, but simply attempting gradual progress within experience.

Another part of the reason may lie in the aesthetic pleasure to be found in meditation (when it is going well). If one manages to attain *dhyana*, or even the preparatory stage of *access concentration*, great feelings of exaltation and deep contentedness can arise. This is naturally something that one then wishes to repeat. However, in my experience, the more you try to repeat a good experience in meditation, the more you will be attached to it, and the less likely the subtle conditions required for a repeat of the earlier experience are to arise. It may be that those who seem hooked on meditation, and not able to see it in perspective, are just continually hunting that elusive experience of pleasure in meditation. However, as any good meditation teacher should tell you, it is better not to meditate in order to seek good experiences, but to seek overall spiritual development.

Nothing I have said here about putting meditation in context, in fact, might not also be said by a good meditation teacher. Buddhism certainly widely recognises the limitations as well as the potentialities of meditation. However, the issue, as ever, is how consistently Buddhist views and attitudes actually reflect that recognition.

Instant enlightenment

The belief in "instant enlightenment" is part of the Zen tradition that through a sudden breakthrough, delusion will instantaneously disappear. Such enlightenment is usually called *satori* or *kensho* in the Zen tradition. What I am interested in here, though, is the relationship of such sudden enlightenment to meditation.

In Zen, the distinction made in other Buddhist schools between *samatha* meditation (which cultivates concentration, including positive emotion, and leads to *dhyana*) and *vipassana* meditation (which leads to insight) is denied. For Zen, an intense aesthetic state such as *dhyana* will contain access to wisdom, so there is no need to cultivate wisdom separately. Instant enlightenment is thus seen also as an aesthetic state which contains spontaneous and intuitive wisdom. One could not prepare for it by thinking of any kind, only by opening the intuition.

Zen meditation practices are thus renowned for their minimalism. In the most basic and common, zazen, one simply experiences the present with awareness, and no other expectations.

The intense usefulness of this practice, which gets one to focus on acceptance of immediate conditions, should not obscure the layer of metaphysical assumptions through which Zen is interpreted. To have an aesthetic experience, however refined, and label it necessarily an insight experience, seems dogmatic, hardly different from having an experience of *dhyana* and labelling it God. The refinement or power of an experience alone will not justify us in claiming to have gained new understanding through it, unless one can also use reason in relation to that understanding.

Change through the Middle Way can only come gradually, for we can only make progress by reaching a new and better stage relative to the last one, and by exercising judgement as to the truth. We do not get closer to the truth (except by accident) by taking a random stab at it reliant on intuition alone, and a deeply absorbed pleasant experience by itself does not get us closer to the truth (though it may set up good conditions for investigation in us). An effort at wisdom is required, which means that the intellect is required. That does not mean that intellectual activity doesn't have limitations, or that they can't be recognised.

Thus, however useful practices such as *zazen* may be when separated from Zen beliefs about instant enlightenment, the overall framework of thinking here seems quite incompatible with the Middle Way, and thus showing a major conflict within Buddhist thought.

Secret sadhanas

Sadhanas are meditation practices, mainly found in the Mahayana (particularly Tibetan Buddhism), that involve the visualisation of a Buddha or bodhisattva figure with prescribed features, in a prescribed way and order, and usually accompanied by the chanting of a mantra. For example there is a sadhana of the Buddha, known in the Mahayana as Shakyamuni, or there is a sadhana of Green or White Tara. The overall goal of such a meditation practice is to help to develop the enlightened qualities of the visualised being in oneself. Sometimes, some practitioners visualise themselves *as* the being, in order to aid this process.

As a practice, this seems to have the same disadvantages as the general tendency in Buddhism to focus on enlightenment as an end result. That is, the various figures are supposed to represent the qualities of a state *of enlightenment*, not the process of getting there or the process of moving from one's present state to a higher state. To practise a sadhana is almost inevitably to dwell on the fixed metaphysical idea of enlightenment, rather than an experiential symbolisation of how to get there.

But of course, we are not actually capable of experiencing visual qualities that are beyond our experience, and there are marked limits to how far visual images can really support dogmas. The artistic images on which sadhanas are based can appeal greatly to our experience. For a while, as a member of the Western Buddhist Order, I visualised the Blue Buddha Akshobhya. The imaginative links made between the colour and the many other particular symbolic associations with Akshobhya (e.g. with elephants) I found fascinating. But surely this was a set of associations set up in my imagination? It had nothing to do with enlightenment, nor did it even particularly symbolise spiritual progress for me. The Five-Buddha mandala, of which Aksobhya forms a part, could symbolise spiritual progress through the integration of the *different* colours and qualities of the different Buddhas, and thus relate more directly and positively to my experience, but I was told that there was no traditional sadhana practice of visualising the whole mandala.

Another way of seeing positive benefits in the practice might be of imitating someone's posture and expression who is in a better state than oneself. By repeatedly visualising someone happier, for example, one might become happier. So, the visualisation of a positive figure might have that good effect – however, again this has nothing to do with them being enlightened, and it might be better just to visualise a photograph of someone you know exhibiting a positive quality you'd like to imitate.

There may be many more benefits of sadhanas than I can explore in this short section, or be aware of given my limited experience of practising one, but they will all uniformly gain their value by a relationship to experience rather than enlightenment. It may well be that these positive effects outweigh the possible negative effects of dwelling constantly on the idea of enlightenment.

The secrecy surrounding sadhanas, however, does not seem to support the likelihood of them being treated as practices that relate to one's experience. Traditionally, at least in Tibetan Buddhism, one needs to be *initiated* into a sadhana practice by a guru, and people who have not received this initiation should not do the practice. This secrecy is in any case becoming increasingly irrelevant when many sadhanas can be read about in books, but the larger point is that it increases the revelatory authority of guru and tradition, when in fact it is an individual who freely chooses to take up (or give up) a sadhana practice.

There is also nothing secret about sadhanas that should stop them being more widely taught for those who wish to learn them, or them being individually modified from the particular strict instructions traditionally given. These are individual meditation practices done for the benefit of an individual, so they should be under that individual's control, not another source of power for traditional pseudo-priesthoods guarding supposed sacred mysteries. The sacredness and specialness of the sadhana, like that of anything else, are found in the experience of the individual, where it is individual imaginative associations that the individual might choose to guard, not the sadhana tradition as a whole.

Mantric mumbo-jumbo

Closely related to the topic of sadhanas is that of mantras, which are used not only in sadhanas, but in more public rituals. Generally mantras are invariable phrases, in Sanskrit or another language, which are chanted, and the chanting of mantras may be used as a kind of concentration or mindfulness practice, in public or in private.

Of course, mantras have had quite a bad press. "Mantra" is often used in English now to mean a meaningless expression which someone repeats because it is the current "in" thing to say in their group. Far from being meaningless, Buddhists claim to find them especially meaningful. Some words found in mantras (such as "padma" or "vajra") have other uses as words referring to objects, so they clearly have a "meaning". Other words ("Ah","Hum" and other such seed-syllables) have no meaning of their own beyond that provided by their associations with a mantra, but of course that doesn't make them meaningless either.

What I can find disturbing about mantras is the way in which they represent the authority of tradition, and the exaggerated claims sometimes made about them. Lama Anagarika Govinda, for example, makes a lot of silly claims about mantras representing the underlying essence of the universe[46]. To be fair, I have rarely heard Buddhists repeating such claims. Nevertheless, they would probably be upset if I were to start introducing other random words in part of the mantra. Why is it better to chant "Om mani padme hum" than "Om mani turnip hum", or for that matter, "turnip carrot spinach beet"? You could imagine those four vegetables generating lots of concentration if recited in the right way.

If tradition carries all the weight of this, and the only reason for chanting mantras in a particular form is tradition, it would be better to break such tradition, if only to make the point that tradition for its own sake has no value. It is much harder for human beings to develop initiative than to simply follow custom and habit, so the ideal therefore should be for them to change what they chant in every ritual and practice,

---

[46] See Lama Anagarika Govinda *The Foundations of Tibetan Mysticism,* Weiser 1969, especially p.22 on 'Om', but also throughout.

maintaining the initiative. At the same time, the power of tradition and its metaphysical baggage might mysteriously slacken.

Chapter 12: The door of wisdom is locked

Some Buddhist readers may be wondering how much of Buddhism is left standing after all this criticism. The answer is actually quite a lot. Not just the Middle Way, but the Noble Eightfold Path and many of the further formulae which develop limbs of that path, such as the Four Right Efforts. The interlocking Threefold Path of morality, meditation and wisdom is left, with a rich fund of meditation practices, wisdom reflections, and inspiring stories. A great deal of Buddhism, fortunately, is completely practical.

The trouble with Buddhism is predominantly one of presentation and language. Very often Buddhists just don't seem to realise, or perhaps don't care about, the hugely off-putting effect their language may be having on non-Buddhists, when the language has only been unthinkingly adopted out of tradition and they could perfectly well put things in a way which is both more acceptable and more coherent.

As an example of this lack of regard for presentation and language, I recently attended the funeral of a friend, a Buddhist and a member of the Western Buddhist Order who died prematurely, so that although the funeral was Buddhist, there were many non-Buddhist members of his family there as well. The words spoken about my friend by many, mainly Buddhists, were moving and sincere and obviously created a good impression on the non-Buddhists present. At the end, at the committal in the crematorium, however, all this goodwill may well have been thrown away at a stroke. The leader said that he didn't know where my friend was now, leaving an appropriate openness about afterlife beliefs that all present could probably share in. Then, finally, he announced a reading from the Tibetan Book of the Dead. Suddenly, it seemed, not only did Buddhism know exactly where my friend would be, it knew exactly what he should be doing as well, as the text offered definite claims about his situation and definite advice for dealing with it. If this was intended to be taken symbolically (symbolically of what?), not a word was said on the subject. One was left with a strong impression both that Buddhists contradicted themselves, and that their regard for those who did not share their traditional ways of understanding things was less than one might have been led to expect.

This is an example of the blare of traditional Buddhism miscommunicating itself and putting people off from its insights in the modern world. In the remainder of this chapter, I am going to look at five particular aspects of the way traditional Buddhism miscommunicates itself and creates barriers to its wisdom.

I haven't unpacked yet

Very often Buddhist teachings seem to tell us something furled-up and concentrated in its traditional form, without unpacking it so that its implications are apparent. Or, if analysis is given, it's not the most relevant sort of analysis. Zen texts are possibly the worst for this. They will go on for hundreds of pages essentially repeating the same point about the intuitive and ungraspable nature of the enlightened state, with stories and paradoxes, but not a word about exactly what one might specifically do that would be helpful to practice, let alone a moral analysis. The Mahayana Perfection of Wisdom texts are very similar.

Here is a typical passage from the *Diamond Sutra:*

Upon the occasion of hearing this Discourse Subhuti had an interior realization of its meaning and was moved to tears. Whereupon he addressed Buddha thus: It is a most precious thing, world honoured one, that you should deliver this supremely profound discourse. Never have I heard such an exposition since of old my eye of wisdom first opened. World-honoured one, if anyone listens to this Discourse of faith with a pure, lucid mind, he will thereupon conceive an idea of Fundamental Reality. We should know that such a one establishes the most remarkable virtue. World-honoured One, such an idea of Fundamental Reality is not, in fact, a distinctive idea; therefore the Tathagata teaches: "Idea of Fundamental Reality" is merely a name.[47]

Typically of Mahayana texts, this text spends a lot of time extolling itself and telling us how profound it is, in a kind of hyper-rhetoric. At the same time as extolling itself, it tells us about its ultimate emptiness in a way that seems calculated to disarm any possible criticism. It is shot full of contradictions, but because the purpose of the text is purely one of emotional manipulation of the reader into the belief that something profound is being

---

[47] Diamond Sutra Section XIV, from *The Diamond Sutra and the Sutra of Hui-Neng*, translated by A.F.Price and Wong Mou-Lam, Shambhala 1969

said, this is assumed not to matter. If Subhuti had already had his eye of wisdom opened he should not be surprised by the Buddha's truisms in the preceding section (where the Buddha has told us that "the world is not really a world"). The truisms are not supposed to be ones of Fundamental Reality, because any such Reality is also being denied, yet nevertheless it is referred to as such. Throughout the text we are told absolutely nothing about the implications of the world not really being a world, or how that might change our judgements or our conduct. Instead windy rhetoric is piled onto windy rhetoric.

What would this text tell us if unpacked? Merely that our judgements may be mistaken, nothing much more than that. This is a point with many important implications, indeed, but the Diamond Sutra tells us about none of them. Yet Buddhists report being profoundly moved by the Diamond Sutra. Sangharakshita reports that he realised he was a Buddhist on reading it at the age of sixteen. One hopes that it was the recognition of the one thing that it has to say that led to his realisation, rather than all the empty rhetoric.

Theravada texts, on the other hand, are often achingly pedestrian rather than overblown. Their oral origins create huge amounts of repetition and formulation, so that often there is only one paragraph or so of actual teachings in a sutta. These teachings are far more likely to be repeated in ten different similes than they are to actually be explained and applied. It would be fruitless here to quote a large section of a sutta in the way that would be required to illustrate this point, but if you examine any of the suttas in the Pali Canon you will see it illustrated. Somebody comes to see the Buddha, with the initial details and context often repeated several times in different ways. The visitor asks a question, and the Buddha gives a response, which is either elaborated into a formula or a set of similes, and perhaps leads to further conversation. It is somewhere in the Buddha's initial response that the actual teaching of the sutta is usually to be found. Sometimes this teaching, having been given first in prose, is then repeated in verse. The visitor is almost invariably impressed or even converted by the Buddha and expresses gratitude for the wisdom offered.

The Buddha's visitors never really succeed in challenging the Buddha, and they are always made to look stupid if they try. The Buddha is not obliged to justify himself further or examine his premises, but merely dispenses wisdom. The suttas are thus not discourses in the same sense of those of Plato, produced not long afterwards but thousands of miles away in Greece, because the topic is not illuminated by a truly critical examination.

Of course, today's Buddhists are not personally responsible for the tediousness of their scriptures. However, they can be held responsible for over-idealising what are really very limited ancient texts, and over-hyping the nuggets of useful information that they actually contain. Instead of critically examining their scriptures, Buddhist teachers sometimes repeat or imitate their tedious and useless features. Whether giving talks or in print, they can spend large amounts of time on irrelevancies, or spend so long warming up that they only reach the main point at the end. One is sometimes told very little about the *implications* of the main point.

There is a long tradition in Buddhism of commenting on the scriptures, but the commentaries are often as voluminous and as useless as the original texts. Instead of commentary, the Buddhist texts need savage editing for a modern audience: but after being cut down to their actual useful content, that useful content (rather than all the attendant contingent matter) then needs to be critically discussed and applied. In effect, the texts need to be totally rewritten, with a quite different kind of amplification of the points they contain. This is a huge job which I have yet to find any Buddhist undertaking, often because of exaggerated respect for the texts as they stand.

I keep repeating myself

Buddhism is full of repetitions. Mantras are repeated many times. The same rituals are done in exactly the same form over and over and over again. The scriptures, particularly from the Pali Canon, repeat themselves due to their oral origins. Insight meditations involve constantly going over the same idea and "turning it over in one's mind". Study leaders also often think it appropriate to repeat study of the same basic points.

People, are, of course, forgetful. Any teacher knows that repeating a point, especially a bit later, can make it much more likely to stick some time later. The psychology of study also suggests that repetition of an idea at intervals is the best way to remember it. Yet often, Buddhist repetition is not just designed to enable better remembrance. The idea is rather that if we keep repeating something we will gain a deeper understanding of it. It is this assumption that seems to me often mistaken.

Human beings crave constant stimulus and variety, so that when events start to turn too predictable, they may switch off through boredom, or start to vote with their feet. To some extent, more subtle levels of interest which defer boredom are a good thing, and mindfulness provides that subtle level of interest in even the simplest things, such as the breath or the surface of a puddle. However, one teaches mindfulness through meditation and aesthetic appreciation, not by boring people. Whilst the repetition of a walk past the same tree every day may be a source of unending delight, the repetition of the same *concepts* or words, only provokes yawns.

Of course, concepts need not be boring at all. Philosophers play with concepts by analysing them, comparing different interpretations, and arguing about their implications and relations to other concepts. The relationship of concepts to examples is also fascinating. Yet, a Buddhist reflection on impermanence, say, does not call for analysis or argument, and though examples are used they do not seem to be the main point. One is somehow supposed to make impermanence part of one's understanding by repeating the concept, mentally or actually, over and over again. In my experience, certainly, this never works, nor have I yet heard a convincing account of how it really works for anyone else.

I have a suspicion that this assumption that the mere repetition of concepts helps one to become wiser is linked to the metaphysical assumptions commonly found in Buddhism. Metaphysics, after all, is a kind of word worship. If you think that the universe is somehow built in relation to a set of words, that describe how things really are, then you can almost magically evoke the universe by using those words. By repeating "impermanence" for example, one magically calls up the impermanence in the universe. However, as I have already argued in chapter one, impermanence is *not* a metaphysical truth about the universe any more than permanence is. There are no short cuts in the recognition of specific ways in which our assumption of permanence (or our assumption of impermanence) may be contributing to our delusion, and no magic words we can use to suddenly summon reality. We need to consider our experiences one by one.

I need an update

Often in Buddhism, teachings, practices or stories from the Buddhist scriptures, or from accounts of other great teachers of the past, are retold on the assumption that they are relevant to the present. It is rare that they are *completely* irrelevant, but they may certainly need a good deal of interpretation to become justifiably relevant today.

Teachings that involve karma, rebirth and past lives certainly form one set that need an update. Just the shift from a context where rebirth is generally believed in to one where it generally isn't, completely changes the meaning of such teachings from (perhaps) basic ethics to metaphysical speculation. If one thinks about why a certain monk in the Pali Canon defends rebirth, for example, the answer may be in terms of concern about basic social morality, and people having a reason to support their neighbours rather than stealing from them. Rebirth certainly has no significance of this kind today.

Another type of teaching that badly needs an update are discussions of the relationship between Buddhism and other philosophies, especially when these draw on the arguments between the Buddha and teachers of other persuasions in the Pali

Canon. I have already discussed the issues behind this in chapter 8. The alternative religions and philosophies that exist today in the West (or even in the East) are totally different from those that existed at the time of the Buddha – the Buddha knew no utilitarianism, no scientific type of materialism, no Marxism, no Christianity, no Islam. Yet all too often I have heard Buddhist speakers simply bundle these modern religions into the categories of "eternalism" and "nihilism" (as traditionally defined), where they fit ill, without further thought. An updating of "eternalism" and "nihilism" are badly needed (indeed I have attempted one myself[48]), but until there is some widely accepted updating by Buddhists on clear grounds, speakers who use these terms in their traditional definitions and expect them to still apply are hardly likely to be understood.

I've got culture-shock

In some ways it is difficult for us to completely distinguish between teachings that are alien because of their distance in the past, and teachings that are alien because of

---

[48] In chapters 3 and 4 of *A Buddhist theory of moral objectivity*: see www.moralobjectivity.net/thesis_index

the cultural gap between the West and India, Tibet, Japan or wherever the teachings come from originally. Very often it is difficult to completely separate the two elements, and they are intermingled. Broadly, teachings with culture-shock are ones that might not go down too badly in that country today, but go down badly in the West – but obviously places like Japan and India are now subject to so much Western influence that the point is a matter of speculation.

There are two examples of culture-shock I'm going to specifically mention: those of magic and those of faith.

Buddhist teachings involving magic are rife. For example, the stories of the mahasiddhas, originally Indian but transmitted via Tibetan Buddhism, are full of magical events, as are the biographies of the great Tibetan gurus such as Marpa and Padmasambhava. Even the normally more staid Pali Canon mentions miracles performed by the Buddha, and has him sheltered from the rain by a snake's hood. The attainment of the fourth dhyana is said to be accompanied by the development of magical (or paranormal) powers such as telekinesis and clairvoyance.

Many of these magical events have a symbolic significance which diffuses Western disbelief, and gives what would otherwise be just a wacky story a real meaning. Some Western teachers are good at pointing out such symbolic significance[49], but it does need pointing out. All too often such stories are just told, even on public occasions with audiences of varying levels of experience. Buddhists who are used to handling symbolism may not be aware quite how literal-minded most people are, and how difficult they often find it to make symbolic interpretations, especially in a culturally alien mythology, without a lot of support.

My other example concerns stories about excessive faith. These may go down a lot better, at least with some audiences, in India, where there is a strong tradition of devotion to gurus, than in the West. Nevertheless, I have often heard such stories just told by Buddhists on public occasions, as if it were obvious that they reflected a way of behaving that everyone should want to follow. One such example from the Pali Canon (Sutta Nipata) is of

---

[49] A good example of this is found in the guide to the symbology of the life of the Buddha found in Sangharakshita *A Guide to the Buddhist Path,* Windhorse (1990)

Pingiya[50], who sings the praises of the Buddha and maintains faith in him, despite living at a great distance from the Buddha, and hardly ever seeing him. Is this kind of faith really appropriate? Does he really know what it is that he is holding in mind so much, and can he really understand the Buddha's teachings with so little instruction? Might it not be better for him to follow someone else near at hand (given that he is living prior to widespread communication at a distance) who could actually provide personal teaching and support? These questions, which might well be there in the background for Westerners, are almost never asked when this story is discussed.

I'm quite familiar really

My final category is of ideas that seem familiar from Western culture, and when encountered in Buddhist teaching immediately get Westerners running in familiar grooves. These friends are false in the sense that, if they are to really get the benefit of what is different in the Buddhist teachings, they need to understand that they are different, or at least that they *should* be

---

[50] Sutta Nipata Ch.5, verses 1131-1149

interpreted differently to be compatible with the Middle Way.

One example is the idea of self-denying love. One can read in the Pali Canon about the disciple who, to be a true disciple of the Buddha, should allow himself to be beaten up, robbed, or even sawed limb from limb by bandits without a word of reproach or a moment of ill-will[51]. Those many Buddhists with Christian backgrounds could hardly refrain from thinking of the crucifixion of Christ here. The implication seems to be that true compassion, like true Christian love, is indifferent to bodily suffering and self-defence, and consists primarily in a masochistic passivity.

This is the gross version, and I have never encountered Buddhists (though I have met Christians) who actually attempted to practice such "love". The subtle version, however, which I think I have detected even in quite experienced Buddhists, is the cultural idea that love is "unselfish" and involves doing one's duty to others even to the extent of denying oneself. There is more discussion of this point in chapter 3. Again, the Buddhist teaching may just spark a pre-

---

[51] "The simile of the saw" from Kakacupama Sutta, Majjhima Nikaya Sutta 21

existent set of ideas, and seem familiar when it really isn't.

My second example is that of nature. In the West there is a long tradition of alternately exploiting and sentimentalising "nature". It is either a resource given to us by God, or a source of cuddly bunny-rabbits peacefully grazing on our favourite patch of down. More recent environmental concerns have created a third view of nature, as a set of interrelationships which is a source of meaning and value. Western Buddhists hearing the idea of dependent origination, especially when interpreted in terms of mutual causality, have read this concept in terms of nature – again this is discussed in chapter 6.

This is another false friend, because dependent origination is in no way the source of the values that have been attributed to "nature" in the West. If anything, it is a process of suffering and hence a source of dread, and its interrelationships are ones that we suffer through our ignorance of. In traditional Buddhism dependent origination is a doctrinal concept explaining the processes of samsara – in my view, as I said in chapter 5, an empty one which makes it all the easier to project onto –

but it is neither a mother goddess nor a source of Wordsworthian nature-mysticism.

Western Buddhism is a situation where many people have imperfectly grasped and digested concepts. It often does not take long poking a "Buddhist" idea to find a Western one underneath, the lines of which have been mysteriously taken by the "Buddhist" one on top. It is a strangely deracinated society, in which ideas that have often not been held very long can be held with as much stubbornness as those held for a lifetime. It is often those Buddhists who are most deeply conservative whose conservatism has its roots in something completely non-Buddhist, such as Platonism, or romantic ideas about traditional societies. Those who are most radical, less afraid of outward western influences, and do not feel much at home in the "Buddhist" group, on the other hand, may in some respects be more Buddhist than the Buddhists.

Whatever Buddhism may be – at its best – it is not all that familiar really. It is those who keep moving into uncharted territory, and are ready to give up the places they already occupy to the savages, who have most closely absorbed the finest insights of Buddhism.

Conclusion

It is not too late to renew Buddhism in the West. It is not too late to agree principles on which to base it that are truly universal. It is not too late to start giving priority to following the Buddha's practical example in taking the Middle Way, rather than his supposed revelation. It is not too late to give up divisive social structures such as orders, monastic or otherwise. It is not too late to restore critical thinking to the crucial place it needs to have in Buddhist practice. It is not too late to start presenting Buddhism to Western society in a more coherent fashion, which actually enables people to understand its core insights.

It may not be too late, but it would still be surprising (though not impossible) if any of these things happen. The vested interests and the habits of thinking are deeply rooted, as with all human beings. There will be many Buddhists who, if they get as far as reading this book, will not understand why I want to say such things about a Buddhist tradition that they find perfectly satisfactory. If change for the better occurs it will probably not be primarily due to existing Buddhists, shallowly bedded though they may be, but due to the many people on the margins.

It is to those people on the margins that this book is primarily addressed. The people who have tried out a couple of meditation classes, or dabbled in a few books about Buddhism. They have tried it a bit, but were not quite happy, and thus not gone into it any further. I have tried to explain here why I think they have very good reasons for not being happy with the Buddhism they encountered. It is these people who are potentially powerful, and who may yet change Buddhism radically – or set up a new version for themselves.

May they succeed in the renewal of Buddhism.

Printed in Great Britain
by Amazon